D1601552

Projective Identification and Psychotherapeutic Technique

COMMENTARY

"Two things you should know about this book: the first is that Dr. Ogden illuminates some of the experiences with patients that we must bear in order to be of help. The second is that Dr. Ogden's writing offers us a sense of the attitudes and aptitudes that are the attainment of such extraordinary clinicians as Elvin Semrad. This latter aspect of the book makes it particularly special, for to deliver in print the feeling and spirit of the finest clinical thinking is a remarkable achievement. The gift is not a common one."

—J. J. Andresen, M.D., in *Contemporary Psychiatry*

"This very interesting book broadens the concept of projective identification and includes rich clinical material illustrating the technique involved in the use of the concept. The major clinical contribution of this book is the focus on the patient's presentation in treatment of an identification with a significant other for purposes of mastering traumatic experiences. The patient's attempts to enmesh the therapist in a role enactment or actualization are illustrated in a number of clinical examples. To Ogden, projective identification involves an interpersonal enactment or actualization. Unconscious feelings are evoked in the other through the process of projection and splitting. . . .

"Ogden proceeds to discuss the concept from its origination by Klein through its use by others, including Bion, Searles, and Langs. He addresses interpretation versus silent containment, and the importance of containing the patient's projections. His chapter, 'Issues of Technique,' provides rich clinical material that illustrates the concept.

"Ogden's thinking on projective identification integrates Klein's, Bion's, and Grotstein's thinking with that of Winnicott. Containment and the holding environment play a large part in Ogden's technical recommendations. Throughout the book he cautions against untimely interpretations that serve more often to ease therapeutic anxiety and distress, and that force material back into the patient that should be held 'in reverie' (Bion) for the patient."

—Janet Schumacher Finell, in *Psychoanalytic Review*

PROJECTIVE IDENTIFICATION AND PSYCHOTHERAPEUTIC TECHNIQUE

Thomas H. Ogden, M.D.

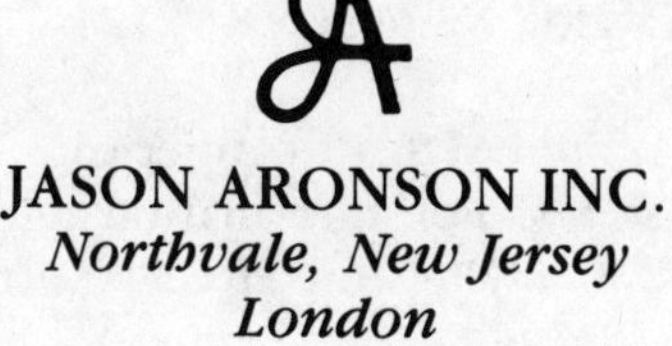

JASON ARONSON INC.
Northvale, New Jersey
London

Credits

Chapter 2 On projective identification. *International Journal of Psycho-Analysis* 60:357–373, 1979.

Chapter 5 A developmental view of identifications resulting from maternal impingements. *International Journal of Psychoanalytic Psychotherapy* 7:486–587, 1978.

Chapter 6 Projective identification in psychiatric hospital treatment. *Bulletin of the Menninger Clinic* 45:317–333, 1981.

Chapter 7 On the nature of schizophrenic conflict. *International Journal of Psycho-Analysis* 61:513–533, 1980.

Chapter 8 Treatment of the schizophrenic state of nonexperience. Written for original publication in *Technical Factors in the Treatment of the Severely Disturbed Patient,* ed. L. B. Boyer and P. L. Giovacchini. In press. New York: Jason Aronson.

New Printing 1991

10 9 8 7 6 5 4 3 2

ISBN 0-87668-446-0 (hardcover)
ISBN-0-87668-542-4 (paperback)

Library of Congress Catalog Number 81-67124

Manufactured in the United States of America. Jason Aronson Inc. offers books and cassettes. For information and catalog, write to Jason Aronson Inc., 230 Livingston Street, Northvale, New Jersey 07647.

To my parents

Contents

Acknowledgments

I wish to express my gratitude to my wife, Sandra, for her insightful comments on many of the issues discussed in this book and for her help in editing the manuscript. I am grateful to her and to my children, Peter and Benjamin, for the patience and love that they have shown in allowing me the time to write this book.

Any clinician working intensively with severely disturbed patients will know that such work is difficult, if not impossible, to do in isolation. I was fortunate to have had the opportunity to do much of the inpatient work described in this volume at the Adolescent and Young Adult Inpatient Service of Mount Zion Hospital and Medical Center, San Francisco. I would like to thank the staff of the service for their dedication and perseverance. I would also like to express my appreciation to Prof. Erik Erikson, who served as clinical consultant to the staff, and to Dr. Otto Will, who served as clinical director for an important period of the life of the ward.

I am glad to have the opportunity to express my gratitude to Dr. James Grotstein and Dr. Bryce Boyer for the warmth they have shown me in the course of providing astute and creative comments on the ideas that I have developed.

Over the past several years, the students who have participated in my object relations theory seminar at Mount Zion Hospital have provided me with an exciting forum in which to explore the clinical and theoretical problems discussed in this book.

Finally, I would like to express deep gratitude to the two

analysts with whom I have worked in the course of my personal analysis.

1
INTRODUCTION

Projective identification is not a metapsychological concept. The phenomena it describes exist in the realm of thoughts, feelings, and behavior, *not* in the realm of abstract beliefs about the workings of the mind. Whether or not one uses the term or is cognizant of the concept of projective identification, clinically one continually bumps up against the phenomena to which it refers—unconscious projective fantasies in association with the evocation of congruent feelings in others. Resistance on the part of therapists and analysts to thinking about these phenomena is understandable: it is unsettling to imagine experiencing feelings and thinking thoughts that are in an important sense not entirely one's own. And yet, the lack of a vocabulary with which to think about this class of phenomena seriously interferes with the therapist's capacity to understand, manage, and interpret the transference. Projective identification is a concept that addresses the way in which feeling-states corresponding to the unconscious fantasies of one person (the projector) are engendered in and processed by another person (the recipient), that is, the way in which one person makes use of another person to experience and contain an aspect of himself. The projector has the primarily unconscious fantasy of getting rid of an unwanted or endangered part of himself (including internal objects) and of depositing that part in another person in a powerfully controlling way. The projected part of the self is felt to be partially lost and to be inhabiting the other person. In association with this unconscious projective fantasy there is an interpersonal interaction by means of which the recipient is pressured to think, feel, and behave in a manner congruent with the ejected feelings and the self- and object-representations embodied in the projective fantasy. In other words, the recipient is pressured to engage in an identification with a specific, disowned aspect of the projector.

The recipient may be able to live with such induced feelings and manage them within the context of his own larger personality system, for example, by mastery through understanding or integration with more reality-based self-representations. In such a case, the projector may constructively reinternalize by introjection and identification aspects of the recipient's handling of the induced feelings. On the other hand, the recipient may be unable to live with the induced feelings and may handle such feelings by means of denial, projection, omnipotent idealization, further projective identification, or actions aimed at tension relief, such as violence, sexual activity, or distancing behavior. In these cases the projector would be confirmed in his belief that his feelings and fantasies were indeed dangerous and unbearable. Through identification with the recipient's pathological handling of the feelings involved, the original pathology of the projector would be further consolidated or expanded.

The concept of projective identification by no means constitutes an entire theory of therapy, nor does it involve a departure from the main body of psychoanalytic theory and technique. It does go significantly beyond what is ordinarily referred to as transference, wherein the patient distorts his view of the therapist while directing toward the therapist the same feelings that he held toward an earlier person in his life (Freud, 1912a, 1914a, 1915d). In projective identification, not only does the patient view the therapist in a distorted way that is determined by the patient's past object relations; in addition, pressure is exerted on the therapist to experience himself in a way that is congruent with the patient's unconscious fantasy.

Projective identification provides a clinical-level theory that may be of value to therapists in their efforts to organize and render meaningful the relationship between their own experience (feelings, thoughts, perceptions) and the transference. It will be seen in the discussion of clinical material that from the perspective of projective identification many of the stalemates and dead-ends of therapy become data for the study of the transference and a medium through which the makeup of the patient's internal object world is communicated.

This definition undoubtedly raises a great many questions. The discussion of these questions will be deferred until the next chapter while at this point only the *form* of the concept will be considered. The concept integrates statements about unconscious fantasy, interpersonal pressure, and the response of a separate personality system to a set of engendered feelings. Projective identification is in part a statement about an interpersonal interaction (the pressure of one person on another to comply with a projective fantasy) and in part a statement about individual mental activity (projective fantasies, introjective fantasies, psychological processing). Most fundamentally, however, it is a statement about the dynamic interplay of the two, the intrapsychic and the interpersonal. The usefulness of many existing psychoanalytic propositions is limited because they address the intrapsychic sphere exclusively and fail to afford a bridge between that sphere and the interpersonal interactions that provide the principal data of the therapy.

As will be discussed, the schizophrenic and, to a lesser extent and intensity, all patients in an interpersonal setting are almost continually involved in the unconscious process of enlisting others to enact with them scenes from their internal object world. The role assigned to the therapist may be the role of the self or the object in a particular relationship to one another. The internal object relationship from which these roles are derived is a psychological construct of the patient's, generated on the basis of: realistic perceptions and understandings of present and past object relationships; misunderstandings of interpersonal reality inherent in the infant's or child's primitive, immature perception of himself and others; distortions determined by predominant fantasies; and distortions determined by the nature of the patient's present modes of organizing experience and thinking, for example, by splitting and fragmentation.

If we imagine for a moment that the patient is both the director and one of the principal actors in the interpersonal enactment of an internal object relationship, and that the therapist is an unwitting actor in the same drama, then projective identification is the process whereby the therapist is given stage directions for a particular role. In this analogy it must be borne in mind that the therapist has not volunteered to play a part and only retrospectively comes to understand that he has been playing a role in the patient's enactment of an aspect of his inner world.

The therapist who has to some extent allowed himself to be molded by this interpersonal pressure and is able to observe these changes in himself has access to a very rich source of data about the patient's internal world—the induced set of thoughts and feelings—which are experientially alive, vivid, and immediate. Yet, they are also extremely elusive and difficult to formulate verbally because the information is in the form of an enactment in which the therapist is participating, and not in the form of words and images upon which the therapist can readily reflect. (The question of the optimal extent of the therapist's participation in this type of interpersonal enactment is a crucial one and will be addressed in detail in succeeding chapters.)

The concept of projective identification offers the therapist a way of integrating his understanding of his own internal experience with that which he is perceiving in the patient. Such an integrated perspective is particularly necessary in work with schizophrenic patients because it safeguards the therapist's psychological equilibrium in the face of what sometimes feels like a barrage of chaotic psychological debris emanating from the patient. The schizophrenic's talk is often a mockery of communication, serving purposes quite foreign to ordinary talk, and often completely antithetical to thought itself (see chapters 7 and 8). Terrific psychological strain is entailed in the therapist's efforts to resist the temptation to denigrate and dismiss his own thoughts while the schizophrenic patient is attacking his and the therapist's capacity to think. Problems involving impairment of the capacity to think are far from abstract philosophical questions for the therapist sitting for long periods of time with the schizophrenic patient. The therapist finds that his own ability to think, perceive, and understand even the most basic therapeutic matters becomes worn down and stagnant in the course of his work. Not infrequently the therapist recognizes that he is unable to bring a single fresh thought or feeling to his work with the patient.

When such therapeutic impasses continue unaltered, the strain within the therapist often mounts to an intolerable level and can culminate in the therapist's fleeing from the patient by shortening the sessions (because "thirty minutes is all the patient can make use of"), or terminating the therapy (because "the patient is not sufficiently psychologically minded to profit from psychotherapy"), or offering "supportive therapy" that consists of an exclusively administrative, task-oriented interaction with the patient. Alternatively, the therapist may retaliate against the patient directly (for example, in the form of intrusive "deep interpretations") or indirectly (for example, by means of emotional withdrawal, breaches of confidentiality, "accidental" lateness to sessions, increases of medication, and so on).

It is easy to be scornful of such behavior on the part of the therapist, but defensive countertherapeutic activity in one form or another is inevitable in any sustained intensive therapeutic work with a schizophrenic patient. If these forms of countertransference acting out are scrutinized by the therapist and prevented from becoming established as accepted aspects of therapy, they usually do not result in irreparable damage to the therapy. This is not to condone countertransference acting out on the part of the therapist. But it should be acknowledged that in the course of intensive psychotherapy with disturbed patients, the therapist will find himself saying things that he regrets. Such errors are rarely talked about with colleagues and almost never reported in the literature.[1] However, from the perspective of projective identification, a given error also represents a specific construction that could only have been generated in precisely the way that it was by means of an interaction between this therapist and this patient at this moment in the therapy. The task of the therapist is not simply to eliminate errors or deviations, but to formulate the nature of the specific psychological and interpersonal meanings that have led the therapist to feel and behave in this particular fashion. As will be seen, much of the clinical material presented in this volume involves analysis of facets of the therapist's behavior and feelings that reflect confusion, anger, frustration, fear, jealousy, self-protectiveness, and so forth, and that no doubt at times constitute therapeutic errors. These feelings, thoughts, and actions are analyzed from the perspective of projective identification in such a way as to allow the therapist not only to acknowledge his own contribution to the interpersonal field but also to understand the ways in which his own feelings and behavior (including his errors) may reflect a specific facet of the transference.

The clinical and theoretical usefulness of the concept of projective identification has suffered from imprecision of definition. Because therapists and analysts have used the term in widely differing ways, the term has been the source of considerable confusion in analytic discussions and in the literature. However, because the concept is uniquely valuable, its theoretical parameters and experiential referents should be refined and precisely

---

[1]Clearly, I am not referring here to actual sexual or aggressive activity on the part of the therapist. These represent extremes that indicate that the therapy is entirely out of control. In such circumstances the patient should be referred to another professional, and it is hoped that the therapist will recognize the need to obtain treatment for himself.

delineated. A contribution to this task will be presented in chapter 2. In that chapter, projective identification will be differentiated from the concepts of projection, introjection, identification, and externalization. Also, the early infantile setting for the development of this psychological process will be discussed, along with the historical background of the idea of projective identification.

Chapter 3 will focus on specific issues of technique. Questions regarding how the therapist determines that he is dealing with a projective identification, how he processes the induced feelings, and how he determines when and in what way to respond will be addressed. In chapter 4 the principles of technique proposed in this volume relating to the clinical handling of projective identification will be contrasted with those espoused by Kleinian analysts, classical analysts, the British Middle Group, and the Modern Psychoanalytic Group of analysts.

A developmental hypothesis will be proposed in chapter 5 regarding the impact of excessive maternal projective identification on the infant's early psychological development. Projective identification constitutes one of the principal modes of communication in the mother–infant "dialogue." However, when a mother relies excessively upon projective identification, not only as a mode of communication but as a mode of defense, the resulting interaction can become pathogenic. Case material is presented from the psychotherapy of a patient who in early childhood developed a specific pathological form of identification as a defensive adaptation to maternal projective identifications.

In the course of this volume, the perspective of projective identification will be applied to various aspects of the psychotherapy of borderline and schizophrenic patients. In chapter 6 the application of the concept of projective identification to the management and treatment of patients in a psychiatric hospital setting will be discussed. Psychotherapeutic work with hospitalized patients demands a mode of thought that integrates an understanding of the patient's intrapsychic state, the countertransference, and the nature of and context for the interpersonal interaction (including the way in which the interaction is influenced by the social-system setting). The special problems arising from the expanded and less well defined therapeutic framework that is necessarily involved in inpatient work are analyzed in terms of reverberating circuits of projective identifications originated by both patients and staff members.

With this clinical, theoretical, and developmental understanding of projective identification as background, the final two chapters are devoted to a formulation of the nature of schizophrenic conflict, an analysis of the place of projective identification in the therapeutic resolution of schizophrenic conflict, and a study of the schizophrenic state of psychic death or "nonexperience."

In chapter 7, schizophrenic conflict is formulated in terms of a conflict between wishes to allow meaning to exist and wishes to avoid pain by destroying all meaning and entering a state of nonexperience. In this state, nothing is attributed emotional significance, everything is interchangeable. Moreover, in schizophrenic conflict, not only are there wishes to destroy meaning, these wishes are enacted in the form of actual self-limitation of mental capacities. The term *actualization* is introduced to refer to specific forms of enactment of unconscious fantasy that lie at the core of both projective identification and schizophrenic conflict.

The state of nonexperience represents a pheomenon quite different from feelings and fantasies of meaninglessness; for the schizophrenic patient in a state of nonexperience, wished-for escape into meaninglessness has been made real by the patient's unconsciously self-imposed paralysis of his own ability to think and to attach meaning to perception. It is not a case of the patient's *feeling as if* life were empty and thinking that nothing matters; the schizophrenic patient in a state of psychological shut-down (nonexperience) has in fact rendered himself incapable of generating meanings of any type, including those of emptiness and meaninglessness.

Data from the first three years of the treatment of a chronic schizophrenic patient will provide a clinical focus for a discussion of four phases of resolution of the schizophrenic conflict: the state of nonexperience, the stage of projective identification, the stage of psychotic experience, and the stage of symbolic thought.

Finally, in chapter 8 there is a discussion of technical and theoretical aspects of the intensive psychotherapy of a blind schizophrenic patient who early in therapy regressed to a nonexperiential state. The therapist's management of the therapy and choice of interventions are informed by the perspective of projective identification in conjunction with the understanding of schizophrenic conflict described above.

Unlike many of the "beliefs" of the different schools of psychoanalytic thought, projective identification is not a construct that one accepts or rejects on the basis of an attraction to a metaphor (such as the notion of psychic energy), a piece of imagery (such as the idea of psychological structure), or the compatibility of an idea with other theoretical or philosophical views (such as the death instinct).

Projective identification is a clinical-level conceptualization with three phenomenological references, all of which lie entirely within the realm of observable psychological and interpersonal experience: (1) the projector's unconscious fantasies (observable through their derivatives, such as associations, dreams, parapraxes, and so forth; (2) forms of interpersonal pressure that are often subtle but verifiable; and (3) countertransference experience (a real, yet underutilized source of analyzable data).

2
THE CONCEPT OF PROJECTIVE IDENTIFICATION

Psychoanalytic theory suffers from a paucity of concepts and language to describe the interplay between phenomena in an intrapsychic sphere and phenomena in the spheres of external reality and interpersonal relations. Since projective identification represents one such bridging formulation, it is to the detriment of psychoanalytic thinking that this concept remains one of the most loosely defined and incompletely understood of psychoanalytic conceptualizations.

PROJECTIVE IDENTIFICATION AS FANTASY AND OBJECT RELATIONSHIP

As discussed in chapter 1, through projective identification the projector has the primarily unconscious fantasy of ridding himself of unwanted aspects of the self; depositing those unwanted parts in another person; and finally, recovering a modified version of what was extruded.

Projective identification will be discussed as if it were a sequence of three phases or steps (Malin & Grotstein, 1966).

However, the notion of there being three aspects of a single psychological event better conveys the sense of simultaneity and interdependence that befits the three aspects of projective identification that will be discussed. In a schematic way, one can think of projective identification as a process involving the following sequence of events. First, there is the unconscious fantasy of projecting a part of oneself into another person and of that part taking over the person from within.[1] Then, there is a pressure exerted through the interpersonal interaction such that the recipient of the projection experiences pressure to think, feel, and behave in a manner congruent with the projection. Finally, after being "psychologically processed" by the recipient, the projected feelings are reinternalized by the projector.

Phase One

The first step of projective identification must be understood in terms of wishes to rid oneself of a part of the self (including one's internal objects), either because that part threatens to destroy the self from within or because one feels that the part is in danger of attack by other aspects of the self and must be safeguarded by being held inside a protective person. This latter psychological use of projective identification was prominent in a schizophrenic adolescent.

> The patient, L., vehemently insisted that he opposed psychiatric treatment and was only coming to his sessions because his parents and the therapist were forcing him to do so. In reality, this 18-year-old could have resisted far more

[1]The term *projection* will be used here to refer to the fantasy of expelling a part of the self that is involved in the first phase of projective identification, as distinct from the type of projection that occurs outside the context of a projective identification. The nature of the difference between projection as an independent process and projection as a part of projective identification will be discussed later in this chapter.

> energetically than he did and had it well within his power to sabotage any treatment attempt. However, it was important for him to maintain the fantasy that all of his wishes for treatment and for recovery were located in his parents and in the therapist, so that these wishes would not be endangered by the parts of himself that he felt were powerfully destructive and intent on the annihilation of his self.

A., a 14-year-old psychotic obsessional patient demonstrates the type of projective identification involving the unconscious fantasy of getting rid of an unwanted, "bad" part of the self by putting it into another person.

> A. frequently talked about wishing to put his "sick brain" into the therapist, who would then have to obsessively add up the numbers on every license plate that he saw and be tormented by fears that every time he touched something that was not his, people would accuse him of trying to steal it. This patient made it clear that his fantasy was not one of simply ridding himself of something; it was also a fantasy of inhabiting another person and controlling him from within. His "sick brain" would in fantasy torment the therapist from within, just as it was currently tormenting the patient.

This type of fantasy is based on a primitive idea that feelings and ideas are concrete objects with lives of their own. These "objects" are felt to be located inside oneself, but capable of being removed and placed in another person, thereby relieving the self of the effects of containing them. The obsessional patient just described would often in the course of a therapy hour turn his head violently to the side in an effort to "shake loose" a given worry.

The fantasy of putting a part of oneself into another person and controlling that person from within reflects a central aspect of projective identification: the projector is operating at least in part at a developmental level wherein there is profound blurring of boundaries between self and object representations. In the projector's fantasy, the recipient experiences the projector's feeling—not merely a similar feeling, but the projector's *actual* feeling—which has been transplanted into the recipient. The projector feels "at one with" (Schafer, 1974) the recipient, whereas in projection, the projector feels estranged from, threatened by, bewildered by, or out of touch with the recipient. The person involved in projection might ask, "Why would anyone act in such an angry way when there is nothing to be angry about? There's something the matter with him." Of course, the contrasting processes are rarely found in pure form; instead, one regularly finds a mixture of the two, with greater or lesser preponderance of feelings of oneness or of estrangement.

Phase Two

In the second phase, the projector exerts pressure on the recipient to experience himself and behave in a way congruent with the unconscious projective fantasy. This is not an imaginary pressure, but rather, real pressure exerted by means of a multitude of interactions between the projector and the recipient. *Projective identification does not exist where there is no interaction between projector and recipient.*

> A 12-year-old inpatient, who as an infant had been violently intruded upon psychologically and physically, highlights this aspect of projective identification. The patient said and did almost nothing on the ward but made her presence powerfully felt by perpetually jostling and bumping into people, especially her therapist. This was generally experienced as infuriating by other patients and by the staff. In the therapy hours (often a play therapy), her therapist said that he felt as if there were no space in the room for him. Everywhere he stood seemed to be her spot. This form of interaction represents a form of object relationship wherein

the patient puts pressure on the therapist to experience himself as inescapably intruded upon. This interpersonal interaction constitutes the induction phase of this patient's projective identification.

The psychotic obsessional patient, A., mentioned earlier consistently generated a type of therapeutic interaction that illuminated the induction phase of projective identification.

> A. was born with pyloric stenosis and suffered from severe projectile vomiting for the entire first month of his life before the condition was diagnosed and surgically corrected. Since then he has imagined himself to be inhabited by attacking presences: scolding parents, burning stomach pains, tormenting worries, and powerful rage over which he feels little or no control. The initial phases of his therapy consisted almost exclusively of his attempts to torment the therapist by kicking the therapist's furniture, repeatedly ringing the waiting room buzzer, and ruminating without pause in a high-pitched whine. All of this invited retaliatory anger on the part of the therapist, and it was to the extent that the therapist experienced feelings of extreme tension and helpless rage that the patient felt momentarily calmed. The patient was fully conscious of both his attempts to make the therapist angry, and the calming, soothing effect that this had on him.

This was an enactment of the patient's fantasy that anger and tension were noxious agents within him that he attempted to get rid of by placing them in the therapist. However, as with his projectile vomiting, there was no simple solution: the noxious agents (anger, food, parents) were also essential for life. Projective identification offered a compromise solution wherein the patient could in fantasy rid himself of the noxious but life-giving objects, while at the same time keeping them alive inside a partially separate object. This solution would have been merely a fantasy without the accompanying object relationship, in which the patient exerted terrific pressure on the therapist to conform to the projective fantasy. When there was evidence of verification of the projection (that is, when the therapist showed evidence of tension and anger), the patient experienced a sense of relief, since that offered confirmation that the noxious but life-giving agents had been both extruded and preserved.

From a family observational viewpoint Warren Brodey (1965) has studied one mode of interaction that serves to generate pressure to comply with a projective fantasy. He describes very vividly the way one member of a family may manipulate reality in an effort to coerce another member into "verifying" a projection. Reality that is not useful in confirming a projection is treated as if it did not exist. (See Zinner & Shapiro, 1972, for corroborating clinical data from work with families of adolescents.) This manipulation of reality and the resultant undermining of reality testing is but one technique in the generation of pressure for compliance with an unconscious projective fantasy.

One further point that needs to be made with regard to the induction of a projective identification is the "or else" that looms behind the pressure to comply with the projective identification. I have described elsewhere (Ogden, 1976, chapter 5) the pressure on an infant to behave in a manner congruent with the mother's pathology, and the ever-present threat that if the infant fails to comply, he would cease to exist for the mother. This threat is the muscle behind the demand for compliance: "If you are not what I need you to be, you don't exist for me," or in other language, "I can see in you only what I put there. If I don't see that, I see nothing." In the therapeutic interaction, the therapist is made to feel the force of the fear of becoming nonexistent for the patient if he ceases to behave in compliance with the patient's projective identification. (See Ogden, 1978a, chapter 6, for a detailed discussion of a therapy revolving around this issue.)

Through the projector's interaction with the recipient, two aspects of the fantasy are verified: (1) the idea that the recipient has the characteristics of the projected aspects of the self, and (2) that the object is being controlled by the projector. In fact, the influence is real, but it is not the imagined absolute control by means of transplanted aspects of the self inhabiting the object; rather, it is an external pressure exerted by means of interpersonal interaction. This brings us to the third phase of projective identification, which involves the psychological processing of the projection by the recipient, and the reinternalization of the modified projection by the projector.

Phase Three

In this phase the recipient experiences himself in part as he is pictured in the projective fantasy. In reality, however, the recipient's experience is a new set of feelings experienced by a person different from the projector. They may approximate those of the projector, but they are not identical: the recipient is the author of his own feelings. Albeit feelings elicited under a very specific kind of pressure from the projector, they are the product of a different personality system with different strengths and weaknesses. This fact opens the door to the possibility that the projected feelings (more accurately, the congruent set of feelings elicited in the recipient) will be handled differently from the manner in which the projector has been able to handle them.

If the recipient can deal with the feelings projected into him in a way that differs from the projector's method, a new set of feelings is generated. This can be viewed as a processed version of the original projected feelings and might involve the sense that the projected feelings, thoughts, and representations can be lived with, without damaging other aspects of the self or of one's valued external or internal objects (cf. Little, 1966). The new experience (or amalgam of the projected feelings plus aspects of the recipient) could even include the sense that the feelings in question can be valued and at times enjoyed. It must be kept in mind that the idea of "successful" processing is a relative one and that all processing will be incomplete and contaminated to an extent by the pathology of the recipient.

This digested projection is available through the recipient's interactions with the projector for internalization by the projector. The nature of this internalization (actually a reinternalization) depends upon the maturational level of the projector and would range from primitive types of introjection to mature types of identification (cf. Schafer, 1968). Whatever the form of the reinternalization process, it offers the projector the potential for attaining new ways of handling feelings that he formerly wished to disavow. To the extent that the projection is successfully processed and reinternalized, genuine psychological growth has occurred.

The following is an example of projective identification involving a recipient more integrated and mature than the projector.

> Mr. K. had been a patient in analysis for about a year, and the treatment seemed to both patient and analyst to have bogged down. The patient repetitively questioned whether he was "getting anything out of it" and stated, "Maybe it's a waste of time—it seems pointless," and so forth. He had always paid his bills grudgingly but had begun to pay them progressively later and later, to the point where the analyst began to wonder if the patient would discontinue treatment, leaving one or two months' bills unpaid. Also, as the sessions dragged on, the analyst thought about colleagues who held 50-minute sessions instead of 55-minute ones, and charged the same fee as himself. Just before the beginning of one session, the analyst considered shortening the hour by making the patient wait a couple of minutes before letting him into the office. All of this occurred without attention being focused on it either by the patient or the analyst. Gradually, the analyst found himself having difficulty ending the sessions on time because of an intense

guilt feeling that he was not giving the patient "his money's worth."

When this difficulty with time had occurred repeatedly over several months, the analyst gradually began to understand his trouble in maintaining the ground rules of the analysis: he had been feeling greedy for expecting to be paid for his "worthless" work and was defending himself against such feelings by being overly generous with his time. With this understanding of the feelings that were being engendered in him by the patient, the analyst was able to take a fresh look at the patient's material. Mr. K.'s father had deserted him and his mother when the patient was 15 months old. Without ever explicitly saying so, his mother had blamed the patient for this. The unspoken shared feeling was that the patient's greediness for the mother's time, energy, and affection had resulted in the father's desertion. The patient developed an intense need to disown and deny feelings of greed. He could not tell the analyst that he wished to meet more frequently because he experienced this wish as greediness that would result in abandonment by the (transference) father and attack by the (transference) mother that he saw in the analyst. Instead, the patient insisted that the analysis and the analyst were totally undesirable and worthless. The interaction had subtly engendered in the analyst an intense feeling of greed, which was felt to be so unacceptable to the analyst that at first he too tried to deny and disown it.

For the analyst, the first step in integrating the feeling of greediness was perceiving himself experiencing guilt and defending himself against his feelings of greed. He could then mobilize an aspect of himself that was interested in understanding his greedy and guilty feelings, rather than trying to deny, disguise, displace, or project them. Essential for this aspect of psychological work was the analyst's feeling that he could have greedy and guilty feelings without being damaged by them. It was not the analyst's greedy feelings that were interfering with his therapeutic work; rather, it was his need to disavow such feelings by denying them and by putting them into defensive activity. As the analyst became aware of, and was able to live with, this aspect of himself and of his patient, he became better able to handle the financial and time boundaries of the therapy. He no longer felt that he had to hide the fact that he was glad to receive money given in payment for his work.

After some time, the patient commented as he handed the analyst a check (on time) that the analyst seemed happy to get "a big, fat check" and that that wasn't very becoming to a psychiatrist. The analyst chuckled and said that it is nice to receive money. During this interchange, the analyst's acceptance of his hungry, greedy, devouring feelings, together with his ability to integrate those feelings with other feelings of healthy self-interest and self-worth, was made available for internalization by the patient. The analyst at this point chose not to interpret the patient's fear of his own greed and his defensive, projective fantasy. Instead, the therapy consisted of digesting the projection and making it available for reinternalization through the therapeutic interaction.

In light of the above discussion, it is worth considering whether this understanding of projective identification may not bear directly on the question of the means by which psychotherapy and psychoanalysis contribute to psychological growth. It may be that the essence of what is therapuetic for the patient lies in the therapist's ability to receive the patient's projections, utilize facets of his own more mature personality system to process the projection, and then make the digested projection available for reinternalization through the therapeutic interaction (Langs, 1976; Malin & Grotstein, 1966; Racker, 1957; Searles, 1963).

THE EARLY DEVELOPMENTAL SETTING

Projective identification is a psychological process that is at once a type of defense, a mode of communication, a primitive form of object relations, and a pathway for psychological change. As a defense, projective identification serves to create a sense of psychological distance from unwanted, often frightening aspects of the self. As a mode of communication, projective identification is a process by which feelings congruent with one's own are induced in another person, thereby creating a sense of being understood by or "at one with" the other person. As a type of object relations, projective identification constitutes a way of being with and relating to a partially separate object. Finally, as a pathway for psychological change, projective identification is a process by which feelings like those that one is struggling with are psychologically processed by another person and made available for reinternalization in an altered form.

Each of these functions of projective identification evolves in the context of the infant's early attempts to perceive, organize, and manage his internal and external experience and to communicate with his environment. The infant is faced with an extremely complicated, confusing, and frightening barrage of stimuli. With the help of a "good-enough" mother (Winnicott, 1952), the infant can begin to organize his experience. In this effort toward organization, the infant discovers the value of keeping dangerous, painful, frightening experiences separate from comforting, soothing, calming ones (Freud, 1920). This kind of "splitting" becomes established as a basic part of the early psychological modes of organization and defense (Jacobson, 1964; Kernberg, 1976). As an elaboration of and support for this mode of organization, the infant utilizes fantasies of ridding himself of aspects of himself (projective fantasies) and fantasies of taking into himself aspects of others (introjective fantasies). These modes of thought help the infant to keep what is psychologically valued separate from, and in fantasy safe from, what is felt to be dangerous and destructive.

These attempts at psychological organization and stability occur within the context of the mother–infant dyad. Spitz (1965) describes the earliest "quasi-telepathic" communication between mother and infant as being of a "coenesthetic" type, wherein sensing is visceral and stimuli are "received" as opposed to being "perceived." The mother's affective state is "received" by the infant and is registered in the form of emotions. The mother also utilizes a coenesthetic mode of communication. Winnicott discusses the state of heightened maternal receptivity that is seen in the mother of a newborn:

> I do not believe it is possible to understand the functioning of the mother at the very beginning of the infant's life without seeing that she must be able to reach this state of heightened sensitivity, almost an illness, and then recover from it. . . . Only if a mother is sensitized in the way I am describing can she feel herself into the infant's place, and so meet the infant's needs. (Winnicott, 1956, p. 302)

It is in this developmental setting that the infant develops the process of projective identification as a mode of fantasy with accompanying object relations that serve both defensive and communicative functions. Projective identification is an adjunct to the infant's efforts at keeping what is felt to be good at a safe distance from what is felt to be bad and dangerous. Aspects of the infant can in fantasy be deposited in another person in such a way that the infant does not feel that he has lost contact either with that part of himself or with the other person.

In terms of communication, projective identification is a means by which the infant can feel understood by making the mother feel what her child is feeling. The infant cannot verbalize his feelings so instead must induce those feelings in the mother.

In addition to serving as a mode of interpersonal communication, projective identification constitutes a primitive type of object relationship, a basic way of being with an object that is psychologically only partially separate. It is a transitional form of object relationship that lies between the stage of the subjective object and that of true object relatedness.

This brings us to the fourth function of projective identification, that of a pathway for psychological change. Let us imagine that a child is frightened by his wish to annihilate anyone who frustrates or opposes him. The child may handle these feelings by unconsciously projecting his destructive wishes into his mother and, through the real interaction with her, engender feelings in her that she is a ruthless, selfish person who wishes to demolish anything standing in the way of the satisfaction of her aims and wishes. For example, the child could exhibit persistently stubborn behavior in many areas of daily activity, by making a major battle out of eating, toileting, dressing, going to sleep at night, getting up in the morning, being left with another caretaker, and so forth. The mother might unrealistically begin to feel that she perpetually storms around the house in a frenzy of frustrated rage ready to kill those that stand between her and what she desires.

A mother who had not adequately resolved her own conflicts about destructive wishes and impulses would find it difficult to live with these feelings. She might attempt to deal with them by withdrawing from and refusing to touch the child. Or she might become hostile, even assaultive or dangerously careless with him. In order to keep the child from becoming the target, the mother might displace or project her feelings onto her husband, parents, employer, or friends. Alternatively, the mother may feel so guilty about or frightened of these feelings of frustration and destruction, that she might become overprotective, never allowing the child to roam out of her sight or be adventurous for fear that he might get hurt. This type of "closeness" may become highly sexualized, for example by the mother's constantly caressing the child in an effort to demonstrate to herself that she is not harming him with her touch.

Any of these modes of dealing with the engendered feelings may result in the confirmation for the child that angry wishes for the demolition of frustrationg objects are dangerous to himself and his valued objects. What would be internalized from the mother in this case would be an even stronger conviction than before that the child must get rid of such feelings. In addition, the child could internalize the mother's pathological methods of handling this type of feeling (for example, excessive projection, splitting, denial, or violent enactment).

On the other hand, good-enough handling of the projected feelings might involve the mother's ability to integrate the engendered feelings with other aspects of herself, for example, her healthy self-interest, her acceptance of her right to be angry and resentful toward her child for standing in the way of what she wants, her confidence that she can contain such feelings without acting on them with excessive withdrawal or retaliatory attack. None of this need be available to the mother's conscious awareness. This act of psychological integration constitutes the processing phase of projective identification. Through the mother's interactions with the child, the processed projection (which involves the sense of the mother's mastery of her feelings of frustration and destructive, retaliatory wishes) would be available to the child for reinternalization.

There is nothing to tie the concept of projective identification to any given developmental timetable. The only requirements are that: (1) the projector (infant, child, or adult) be capable of projective fantasy (albeit often very primitive in its mode of symbolization) and specific types of object-relatedness that are involved in the induction and reinternalization phases of projective identification, and (2) that the object of the projection be capable of engaging in the type of object-relatedness that is involved in receiving a projection and of processing the projection. At some point in development, the infant becomes capable of these psychological tasks, and only at that point is the concept of projective identification applicable.

AN HISTORICAL PERSPECTIVE

Melanie Klein introduced the term *projective identification* in "Notes on Some Schizoid Mechanisms" (1946) and applied it to a psychological process arising in the paranoid-schizoid phase of development, wherein "bad" parts of the self are split off and projected into another person in an effort to rid the self of one's "bad objects," which threaten to destroy the self from within. These bad objects (psychological representations of the death instinct) are projected in an effort to "control and take possession of the object."

The only other paper in which Klein discusses projective identification at any length is "On Identification" (1955). In that paper, by means of a discussion of "If I Were You," a story by Julian Green, Klein offers a vivid account of the subjective experience involved in the process of projective identification. In Green's story, the devil grants the hero the power to leave his own body and enter and take over the body and life of anyone he chooses. Klein's description of the hero's experience in projecting himself into another person captures the sense of what it is like to inhabit someone else, control that person, and yet not totally lose the sense of who one really is. It is the sense of being a visitor in the other person, but also of being changed by the experience in a way that will make one forever different. In addition, this account brings home an important aspect of Klein's views: the process of projective identification leaves the projector impoverished until the projected part is successfully reinternalized. The attempt to control another person and have that person act in congruence with one's fantasies requires tremendous vigilance and a very great expenditure of psychological energy, which leaves the projector psychologically depleted.

Wilfred Bion (1959a, 1959b) has made important steps in elaborating upon and applying the concept of projective identification. He views projective identification as the single most important form of interaction between patient and therapist in individual therapy, as well as in groups of all types. Bion's strongly clinical perspective is helpful in emphasizing an aspect of this process that is not clearly elucidated by Klein: "The analyst feels that he is being manipulated so as to be playing a part, no matter how difficult to recognize, in somebody else's phantasy" (1959a, p. 149).

Bion insists that projective identification is not only a fantasy but a manipulation of one person by another and thus an interpersonal interaction. His work manages to capture some of the strangeness and mystery that characterize the experience of being involved as the recipient of a projective identification, which, he suggests, is like having a thought that is not one's own (Bion, 1977b). He also describes the adverse effects of a parent's failure to allow himself to receive the projective identifications of a child or a child's inability to allow his parent to function in this way:

> Projective identification makes it possible for [the infant] to investigate his own feelings in a personality powerful enough to contain them. Denial of the use of this mechanism, either by the refusal of the mother to serve as a repository for the infant's feelings, or by the hatred and envy of the patient who cannot allow the mother to exercise this function, leads to a destruction of the link between infant and breast and consequently to a severe disorder of the impulse to be curious on which all learning depends. (Bion, 1959, p. 314)

Essential aspects of normal development are the child's experience of his parents as people who can safely and securely be relied upon to act as containers for his projective identifications together with his ability to successfully utilize them as such.

Herbert Rosenfeld contributed several important early papers (1952a, 1954) on the clinical applications of projective identification theory to schizophrenia. In particular, he used the concept to trace the genetic origins of depersonalization and confusional states.

Even though the term *projective identification* is not often used by members of other schools of analytic thought, the work of non-Kleinians has been fundamental to the development of the concept. For example, although Donald Winnicott rarely used the term in his writing, much of his work is a study of the role of maternal projective identifications in early development, and of its implications for both normal and pathological development. (See, for example, his concepts of impingement and mirroring [1952, 1967].)

Michael Balint's account (1952, 1968) of his handling of therapeutic regression, especially in the phase of treatment that he calls the "new beginning," focuses very closely on technical considerations which have direct bearing on the handling of projective identifications. Balint cautions us against having to interpret or in other ways having to act on the feelings the patient elicits; instead, the therapist must "accept," "feel with," "tolerate," and "bear with" the patient and the feelings with which he is struggling and asking the therapist to recognize.

> The analyst is not so keen on "understanding" everything immediately, and in particular, on "organizing" and changing everything undesirable by his correct interpretations; in fact, he is more tolerant towards the patient's sufferings and is capable of bearing with them—i.e., of admitting his relative impotence—instead of being at pains to "analyze" them away in order to prove his therapeutic omnipotence. (1968, p. 184)

I would view this in part as an eloquent statement on the analyst's task of being receptive to the patient's projective identifications without having to act on these feelings.

Harold Searles enriches the language that we have for talking about the way a therapist (or parent) must be receptive to the projective identifications of the patient (or child). In "Transference Psychosis in the Psychotherapy of Schizophrenia," Searles explains the importance of the therapist's refraining from rigidly defending himself against experiencing aspects of the patient's feelings.

> The patient develops ego-strengths . . . via identification with the therapist who can endure, and integrate into his own larger self, the kind of subjectively non-human part-object relatedness which the patient fosters in and needs from him. (1963, p. 698)

Searles adds,

> The extent to which the therapist feels a genuine sense of deep participation in the patient's "delusional transference" relatedness to him during the phase of therapeutic symbiosis . . . is difficult to convey in words; it is essential that the therapist come to know that such a degree of feeling-participation is not evidence of "counter-transference psychosis," but rather is the essence of what the patient needs from him at this crucial phase of the treatment. (1963, p. 705)

Searles is here presenting a view that therapy, at least in certain phases of regression, can progress only to the extent that the therapist can allow himself to feel (with diminished intensity) what the patient is feeling, or in the terminology of projective identification, to allow himself to be open to receiving the patient's projections. This "feeling-participation" is not equivalent to becoming as sick as the patient because the therapist, in addition to receiving the projection, must process it and integrate it into his own larger personality and make this integrated experience available to the patient for reinternalization. In a more recent article, "The Patient as Therapist to the Analyst" (1975), Searles describes in detail the opportunity for growth in the analyst that is inherent in his struggle to remain open to the patient's projective identifications.

There is a growing body of literature clarifying the concept of projective identification and integrating the concept into a non-Kleinian psychoanalytic framework. Malin and Grotstein

(1966) present a clinical formulation of projective identification, making this very bulky concept more manageable by discussing it in terms of three elements: the projection, the creation of an "alloy" of external object and projected self, and reinternalization. These authors present the view that therapy consists of the modification of the patient's internal objects by the process of projective identification. Interpretation is seen as a way in which the patient can be helped to observe "how his projections have been received and acknowledged by the analyst" (p. 29).

Finally, I would like to mention the work of Robert Langs (1975, 1976), who is currently involved in the task of developing an adaptational-interactional framework of psychotherapy and psychoanalysis. His efforts represent a growing sense of the importance and usefulness of the concept of projective identification as a means of understanding the therapeutic process. Langs contends that analytic theory must shift from viewing the analyst as primarily a screen to viewing him as a "container for the patient's pathological contents who is fully participating in the analytic interaction" (1976). By making such a shift, we clarify the nature of the therapist's response to the patient's transference and nontransference material and are in a better position to do the self-analytical work necessary for the treatment of the patient, in particular for the correction of errors in technique. For Langs, projective identification is one of the basic units of study within an interactional frame of reference.

TECHNICAL AND THEORETICAL IMPLICATIONS

Interpretation vs. Silent Containment

What does a therapist do when he observes that he is experiencing himself in a way that is congruent with his patient's projective fantasy, that is, when he is aware that he is the recipient of his patient's projective identification? One answer to this question is that the therapist "does" nothing; instead, the therapist attempts to live with the engendered feelings without denying or in other ways trying to get rid of them. This is what is meant by making oneself open to receiving a projection. It is the task of the therapist to contain the patient's feelings.

For example, when the patient is feeling hopelessly unlovable and untreatable, the therapist must be able to bear the feeling that the therapist and the therapy are worthless for this hopeless patient, and yet at the same time not act on the feelings by terminating the therapy (cf. Nadelson, 1976). The "truth" that the patient is presenting must be treated as a transitional phenomenon (Winnicott, 1951) wherein the question of whether the patient's "truth" is reality or fantasy is never an issue. As with any transitional phenomenon, it is both real and unreal, subjective and objective, at the same time. In this light, the question "If the patient can never get better, why should the therapy continue?" never needs to be acted upon. Instead, the therapist attempts to live with the feeling that he is involved in a hopeless therapy with a hopeless patient and is, himself, a hopeless therapist. This, of course, is a partial truth, which the patient experiences as a total truth, and which must be experienced by the therapist as emotionally true just as the good-enough mother must be able to share the truth in her child's feelings about the comforting and life-giving powers of his piece of satin. It would not occur to an empathic mother to ask her child whether his piece of satin *really* can make things better.

Several further aspects of the handling of projective identification must be considered. First, the therapist is not simply an empty receptacle into which the patient can "put" projective identifications. The therapist is a human being with a past, a repressed unconscious, and a personal set of conflicts, fears, and psychological difficulties. The feelings that patients struggle with are highly charged, painful, conflict-laden areas of human experience for the therapist as well as for the patient. It is hoped that the therapist, because of greater psychological integration resulting from his own developmental experience and analysis, is less frightened of, and less prone to run from, these feelings than is the patient. However, we are not dealing with an all-or-nothing phenomenon here, and the handling of the feelings projected by the patient requires considerable effort, skill, and "strain" (Winnicott, 1960a) on the part of the therapist. The therapist's theoretical training, personal analysis, experience, psychological-mindedness, and psychological language are major tools that can all be brought to bear on the experience he is attempting to understand and to contain.

How much of the therapist's understanding of the patient's projective identification should be interpreted to the patient? The therapist's ability not only to understand but also to verbalize his understanding clearly and precisely is basic to therapeutic effectiveness (Freud, 1914a; Glover, 1931). In the case of projective identifications, this is so not only because well-timed clarifications and interpretations may be of value to the patient, but equally because these understandings are essential to the therapist's effort to contain the engendered feelings.

However, the therapist's understanding may at times constitute a correct interpretation *for the therapist* but may not be at all well-timed for the patient. In this case, the interpretation should remain "a silent one" (Spotnitz, 1969), that is, formulated in words in the therapist's mind, but not verbalized to the patient. The silent interpretation can contain much more self-analytic material than one would include in an interpretation offered to the patient. Continued self-analysis in this way is invaluable in a therapist's attempts to struggle with, contain, and grow from the feelings patients are eliciting in him.

There is a danger that the therapist may be tempted to use the patient's therapy exclusively as an arena in which to find help with the therapist's own psychological problems. This can result in a repetition for the patient of an early pathogenic interaction (frequently reported in the childhood of pathologically narcissistic patients) wherein the needs of the mother were the almost exclusive focus of the mother–child relationship. (See Ogden,

1974, 1976, 1978a for further discussion of this form of mother–child interaction.)

Failure to Contain the Projective Identification

Errors in technique very often reflect a failure on the part of the therapist to contain the patient's projective identification adequately. Either through an identification with the patient's methods of handling the projected feelings or through reliance on his own customary defenses, the therapist may come to rely excessively on denial, splitting, projection, projective identification, or enactment, in an effort to defend against the engendered feelings. This basically defensive stance can result in "therapeutic misalliances" wherein the patient and therapist "seek gratification and defensive reinforcements in their relationship" (Langs, 1975, p. 80). In order to support his own defenses, the therapist may introduce deviations in technique, and may even violate the basic ground rules and framework of psychotherapy and psychoanalysis, for example, by extending the relationship into social contexts, giving gifts to the patient, or encouraging the patient to give the therapist gifts, or breaching the code of confidentiality. Failure to adequately process a projective identification is reflected in the therapist's response in one of two ways: either by his mounting a rigid defense against awareness of the feelings engendered, or allowing the feeling or the defense against it to be translated into action. Either type of failure results in the patient's reinternalization of the original projected feelings, combined with the therapist's fears about and inadequate handling of those feelings. The patient's fears and pathological defenses are reinforced and expanded. In addition, the patient may despair about the prospect of being helped by a therapist who shares significant aspects of the patient's pathology.

The therapist's failure to contain the patient's projective identifications is often a reflection of what Grinberg (1962) calls "projective counteridentification." In this form of response to projective identification, the therapist, without consciously being aware of it, *fully* experiences himself as he is portrayed in the patient's projective fantasy. The therapist feels unable to prevent himself from being what the patient unconsciously wants him to be. This differs from being therapeutically receptive to a patient's projective identification because in the latter case the therapist is aware of the process and only partially, and with diminished intensity, shares the patient's unconsciously engendered feelings. The successful handling of projective identification is a matter of balance: the therapist must be sufficiently open to receive the patient's projective identification and yet maintain sufficient psychological distance from the process to allow for effective analysis of the therapeutic interaction.

The Therapist's Projective Identifications

Just as the patient can apply pressure to the therapist to comply with projective identifications, the therapist can put pressure on the patient to validate the therapist's own projective identifications. For example, therapists have an intricately overdetermined wish for their patients to "get better" and this is often the basis for an omnipotent fantasy that the therapist has turned the patient into the wished-for patient. Very often the therapist, through his own projective identification, can exert pressure on the patient to behave as if he were a wished-for "cured" patient. A relatively healthy patient can often become aware of this pressure and alert the therapist to it by saying something like, "I'm not going to let you turn me into another of your successes." This kind of statement, however overdetermined, should alert the therapist to the possibility that he may be engaged in projective identification, and that the patient has successfully processed these projections. It is far more damaging when the patient is unable to process a projective identification in this way and either complies with the pressure (by becoming the "ideal" patient) or rebels against the pressure (by an upsurge of resistance or by termination of therapy).

Winnicott (1947) also reminds us that therapists' and parents' wishes for their patients and children are not exclusively for cure and growth. There are also hateful wishes to attack or annihilate the patient or child (see also Maltsburger & Buie, 1974). A stalemated therapy, a perpetually silent patient, or a flurry of self-destructive or violent activity on the part of the patient may all be signs of the patient's efforts to comply with a therapist's projective identification that involves an attack upon or the annihilation of the patient. As Winnicott suggests, it is imperative that parents and therapists be able to integrate their anger and murderous wishes toward their children and patients without acting upon, denying, or projecting these feelings. Persistent and unchanging projective identifications on the part of the therapist should, if recognized, alert the therapist to a need to seriously examine his own psychological state and possibly to seek further analysis.

Related Psychological Processes

It is important to clarify the relationship of projective identification to a group of related psychological processes: projection, externalization, introjection, and identification. (The relationship of projective identification to the concepts of transference and countertransference will be dealt with in chapters 3 and 8.)

Projection

A distinction must be drawn between the projective mode of thought involved in projective identification and that in projection as an independent process. In the former, the projector subjectively experiences a feeling of oneness with the recipient with regard to the expelled feeling, idea, or self-representation. By contrast, in *projection* the aspect of the self that is in fantasy expelled is disavowed and attributed to the recipient. The projector does not feel kinship with recipient; on the contrary, the recipient is often experienced as foreign, strange, and frightening.

Externalization

The concept of *externalization* (as discussed by Brodey, 1965) refers to a specific type of projective identification wherein there is a manipulation of reality in the service of pressuring the object to comply with the projective fantasy. However, in a broader sense, there is "externalization" in every projective identification, in that the projective fantasy is moved from the internal arena of psychological representations, thoughts, and feelings to the external arena of other human beings and the projector's interactions with them. Rather than simply altering the *psychological representation* of an external object, in projective identification one attempts to, and often succeeds in, effecting specific alterations in the feeling-state and behavior of *another person.*

Introjection and Identification

Just as a projective mode of thought, as opposed to projection, can be seen as underlying the initial phase of projective identification, one can understand the third phase as being based on an introjective mode, as opposed to introjection. In the final phase of projective identification, the individual imagines himself repossessing an aspect of the self that has been "reposing" in another person (Bion, 1959b). In conjunction with this fantasy is a process of internalization wherein the recipient's method of handling the projective identification is perceived, and there is an effort to make this aspect of the recipient a part of the self.

Following the schema outlined by Schafer (1968), introjection and identification are seen as types of internalization processes. Depending upon the projector's maturational level, the type of internalization process employed may range from primitive introjection to mature types of identification. In introjection, the internalized aspect of the recipient is poorly integrated into the remainder of the personality system and is experienced as a foreign element ("a presence") inside the self. In identification, there is a modification of motives, behavior patterns, and self-representations, in such a way that the individual feels that he has become "like" or "the same as" the recipient with regard to a given aspect of that person. So the terms *introjection* and *identification* refer to types of internalization processes that can operate largely in isolation from projective processes or as a phase of projective identification.

SUMMARY

This chapter presents a clarification of the concept of projective identification through a delineation of the relation of fantasy to object relations that is entailed in this intrapsychic-interpersonal process. Projective identification is viewed as a group of fantasies and accompanying object relations involving three phases which together make up a single psychological unit. In the initial phase, the projector unconsciously fantasies getting rid of an aspect of the self and putting that aspect into another person in a controlling way. Secondly, via the interpersonal interaction, the projector exerts pressure on the recipient to experience feelings that are congruent with the projection. Finally, the recipient psychologically processes the projection and makes a modified version of it available for reinternalization by the projector.

Projective identification, as formulated here, is a process that serves as: (1) a type of defense by which one can distance oneself from an unwanted or internally endangered part of the self, while in fantasy keeping that aspect of the self alive in the recipient; (2) a mode of communication by which the projector makes himself understood by exerting pressure on the recipient to experience a set of feelings similar to his own; (3) a type of object-relatedness in which the projector experiences the recipient as separate enough to serve as a receptacle for parts of the self but sufficiently undifferentiated to maintain the illusion of literally sharing the projector's feeling; (4) a pathway for psychological change by which feelings similar to those which the projector is struggling with are processed by the recipient, thus allowing the projector to identify with the recipient's handling of the engendered feelings.

3

ISSUES OF TECHNIQUE

As with the concept of transference, projective identification provides a context for understanding clinical phenomena but does not dictate a specific technique with which the therapist communicates his understanding. Kleinian, the British Middle Group, the Modern Psychoanalytic Group, and classical analysts are in agreement on the centrality of the concept of transference to psychoanalytic work; nevertheless, the technique employed by each of these groups in the analysis of the transference varies significantly. Similarly, the concept of projective identification provides a framework for thinking about the clinical phenomena occurring in psychotherapy and psychoanalysis, but the therapist's mode of intervention will be determined by an additional set of principles constituting this theory of technique: the clinical material that should be addressed first (conscious, preconscious, or unconscious, defense or wish, surface or depth, early or late developmental level, etc.); the timing of the intervention; the form of the intervention (verbal interpretation, confrontation, clarification, questions, silent interpretation, alteration in management of the framework of the therapy, etc.).

In this chapter, a set of principles related to the technical aspects of handling projective identification in psychoanalytic psychotherapy will be presented. Case material will be offered in which the operational use of these principles of technique is demonstrated and discussed.[1] In chapter 4 the mode of handling projective identification presented here is compared with the theories of technique espoused by analysts of the classical, Kleinian, British Middle Group, and Modern Psychoanalytic groups.

Despite the fact that a specific therapeutic technique is not intrinsic to the concept of projective identification, an understanding of the therapeutic process is inherent in the concept. The idea that there is something therapeutic about the therapist's containment of the patient's projective identifications is based upon an interpersonal conception of individual psychological growth: one learns from (in fantasy, "takes in qualities of") another person on the basis of interactions in which the projector ultimately takes back (reinternalizes) an aspect of himself that has been integrated and slightly modified by the recipient. The patient learns from that which was his to begin with. In discussing psychoanalytic technique, Freud (1913) proposed a similar idea about that which the patient can take in from the analyst's interpretations. He stated that the analyst should not offer an interpretation until the patient "is already so close to it that he has only one short step more to make in order to get hold of the explanation himself" (p. 140).

The therapeutic technique for the handling of projective identification discussed in this chapter and elsewhere in the volume is designed *to make available to the patient in a slightly modified form that which was already his but had been formerly unusable for purposes of integration and psychological growth.* At certain junctures in a psychotherapy this goal is best achieved by means of verbal interpretation. Some of the factors that determine when one is at such a point in therapy will be discussed in this chapter, as well as some of the forms such interpretation may take. However, verbal interpretation is not the only way in which the therapeutic goal outlined above is achieved, even in

---

[1]I am grateful to Drs. Michael Bader, Adele Levin, and Stanley Ziegler for allowing portions of their clinical work to be discussed in this volume.

work with relatively healthy patients. For parts of our work with more disturbed patients, verbal interpretation will play a relatively small role.[2]

In work with patients who are dealing predominantly with whole-object-related forms of transference,[3] the therapist's well-timed verbal interpretation will frequently constitute the needed modification of that which was already an aspect of the patient. However, when the patient is dealing with preverbal part-object-related forms of transference, verbal interpretations are often experienced as alien and having little to do with the patient. This is true not only of incorrect or poorly timed interpretations but of any and all attempts to use language for the purpose of understanding meanings. That endeavor (to understand personal meanings) in itself is taken as the hallmark of the therapist and therefore not a reflection of the patient. Under such circumstances, the patient is faced with the dilemma of either (1) attempting to retain a sense of connectedness with the therapist by introjecting the interpretation even though he does not feel as if it is his own, or (2) rejecting the interpretation at the risk of feeling utterly alone and disconnected from the therapist. Usually when the patient internalizes the interpretation in an undigested form, he will feel that he has been forced to, or has chosen to, give

[2]It should be kept in mind that even if a noninterpretive approach is taken for part or all of a therapy, the work may still be psychoanalytic. In discussing the history of the psychoanalytic movement, Freud (1914c), stated that in his view a therapy is psychoanalytic if it takes as its starting point an understanding of transference and resistance.

[3]The term *whole object* refers to one's experience of another person as separate from oneself (i.e. having life as well as feelings and thoughts that are independent of oneself) and continuing to be that same person despite shifts in one's feelings about the other person. The term *part object* refers to a more primitive perception of another person. Aspects of the object are experienced as existing automomously. For example, the frustrating aspect of the mother is experienced as constituting a person that is distinct from the nurturant aspect of the mother. The object is not experienced as entirely separate from oneself and is usually felt to be within one's omnipotent control (e.g. the object can be magically destroyed and re-created).

up his own individual existence and instead has become the therapist in a literal way. Often the patient will at some point (frequently after termination or disruption of therapy) renounce the therapist as dangerous, self-serving, annihilating, and so forth.

Patients who have responded to verbal interpretation by having to ward off the therapist even at the price of feeling completely detached from him often seem to the therapist so walled-off and thickly defended that the therapist experiences corresponding feelings of isolation, frustration, and futility. Even the most accurate, well-dosed, and well-timed interventions seem to make no difference to the patient. Other patients gratefully accept the therapist's interpretations and seem not only to understand them but to build upon them; it is thus all the more disappointing for the therapist to admit to himself after years of work that the patient has not changed (Khan, 1969; Winnicott, 1963).

It must be borne in mind that the perspective of projective identification neither requires nor excludes the use of verbal interpretation; the therapist attempts to find a way of talking with and being with the patient that will constitute a medium through which the therapist may accept unintegrable aspects of the patient's internal object world and return them to the patient in a form that the patient can accept and learn from.

The comments that follow about psychotherapeutic technique are in no sense meant as prescriptions; instead, they are intended to illustrate ways of working within the framework delineated by the understanding of the relationship between projective identification and psychological change that has just been discussed. (In this chapter, only patient-initiated projective identifications are discussed; management of therapist-initiated projective identifications is discussed in chapter 6.)

Issues of Technique

CLINICAL RECOGNITION OF PROJECTIVE IDENTIFICATION

In the clinical application of the concept of projective identification, one question that arises is: How does the therapist know when he has become the recipient of the patient's projective identification? It should certainly be considered as a possibility when the therapist begins to suspect that he has developed an intensely held but highly limited view of himself and the patient that is in an important sense shared by the patient. In other words, the therapist discovers that he has been playing a role in one of the patient's unconscious fantasies (Bion, 1959a). This "discovery" is necessarily to some extent a retrospective judgment, since the therapist's unconscious participation in this interpersonal construction must precede its recognition.

Because of the therapist's unconscious participation in projective identification, the meaning of this type of intrapsychic-interpersonal event is usually not easy to discern and is more easily perceived and understood by those outside of it (for example, by consultants and colleagues). The therapist's task of disentangling himself from a patient's projective identification can at times involve the pain of acknowledging to himself that he has been "drawn into" an enactment of aspects of the patient's pathology.

> An experienced therapist had been treating an adolescent patient on a long-term inpatient unit for about 18 months when he presented his work at a case conference. He concluded from his experience with the patient that she could not be helped because of her intense need to defeat and punish herself. This need was enacted in an endless series of suicidal gestures and extended elopements from the hospital, as well as bizarre and potentially dangerous sexual exhibitionism and promiscuity. The therapist emphasized the "reality" that persistence in treating this patient would

be a misuse of a hospital bed, which could be better utilized by another patient. Furthermore, the hospital itself might suffer if treatment of the patient were continued because of the risk of adverse publicity from the patient's sexual and self-destructive behavior. The therapist stated this to the conference with conviction and with a feeling of having resigned himself to the inevitable transfer of the patient to a state hospital. There was visible dismay and considerable impatience displayed by the therapist when the inevitability of the patient's transfer was questioned by fellow staff members.

Much of the first 18 months of therapy had consisted of a powerful communication by means of evocation of feelings in the therapist. In order to feel any degree of connectedness with the therapist, this patient felt it necessary that the therapist feel her feelings, have her "knowledge" that the deepest truth (in reality, a partial truth) about the patient was that she could never be helped because her insanity would consume and defeat anyone who dared to come within its range. The therapist had become the receptacle for these feelings and experienced them not only as his own, but as indelible and absolute truth.

In the course of the discussion, the therapist was gradually able to understand the therapeutic impasse as an externalization by the patient of a powerfully influential set of internalized early object relations, in which the patient's mother had viewed the patient as the embodiment of her own primitive insane self and as an immediate threat to her own fragilely held sanity.

An ongoing dialogue with a supervisor, consultant, or colleague is often an indispensable adjunct to work with very disturbed patients because of the difficulty of the psychological work entailed in the process of recognizing one's unconscious participation in a patient's projective identification. The development of this type of unconsciously shared, inflexible, largely unquestioned view of oneself in relation to the patient is one of the hallmarks of projective identification.

The therapist's experience while serving as an object of a borderline or schizophrenic patient's projective identification may be contrasted with the experience of treating relatively well integrated patients. In the treatment of relatively healthy patients, the therapist is frequently able to maintain a flexible and relatively detached psychological state of "evenly suspended attention" (Freud, 1912b), although I feel that it is a myth that even quite healthy neurotic patients routinely allow the therapist such freedom. The therapist of the neurotic patient does at times experience an emotional distance from the patient that allows him to listen with the secure knowledge that he does not share in the patient's feelings, ideas, and problems. The therapist has the freedom to try out one identification and then another, for example, identifying for a time with the patient as he recounts an incident in which he has been subtly sadistic to his child and then, moments later, with the child's attempts to deny and defuse the hostility of the parent. Having tried on for size successive aspects of what the neurotic patient is feeling and thinking, the therapist is free to focus his attention (and at times the patient's attention) upon one facet or another of the clinical material.

The following segment from the psychotherapy of a successful businessman in his late thirties demonstrates qualities of a therapeutic relationship in which the therapist is able to view the patient from a secure and reliable psychological distance, that is, from a vantage point of clear self–object differentiation.

> The patient, Mr. B., suffering from a neurotic fear of death as well as other obsessional thoughts, had several days earlier been informed that the advertising agency where he had worked for over 11 years would be folding. After receiving the news, the patient cried during much of each session and said that he did not know what he would do or how he would support himself and his family. "Certainly I won't be able to continue to pay for therapy." In addition to the

reality-based components of the patient's thoughts and feelings, the therapist recognized irrational transference elements in what was occurring.

During his childhood, Mr. B. had elicited anxious concern from his ordinarily very busy mother, an internist, by means of psychosomatic illnesses, phobias, and other forms of distress. The therapist understood the present situation in part as a transference reenactment in which the patient was attempting to elicit a display of concern from the therapist whom the patient now viewed as cold and self-absorbed. The therapist, although not unmoved by the patient, did not feel any urgent need to comfort him. It was not difficult for the therapist to direct his attention to the task of interpreting the patient's need to repeat with the therapist an infantile form of relatedness that the patient, through previous work in the therapy, had already come some distance in understanding and relinquishing.

The distortion of the patient's view of the therapist represented a projection of aspects of his unconscious conception of his mother onto his current perception of the therapist. Had this been a projective identification, the patient would have unconsciously attempted to change not only his view of the therapist but also the therapist himself. There would have been considerable interpersonal pressure exerted on the therapist to engage in a less well differentiated form of relatedness and to share in the patient's distress (as his mother had), as if the loss of the job were as much the therapist's problem as the patient's. The therapist might have begun to feel moved to give advice or consider lowering the fee in order to "save the therapy." In the therapy of the neurotic patient being described, the therapist could rely on the patient's ability to observe and understand the wishes underlying his plaintive form of relatedness to the therapist. The patient himself was eventually able to point out the way he had preconsciously kept information from the therapist that would have made it clear that the patient's prospects were not nearly as bleak as he made them seem.

The following vignette, from the psychotherapy of a borderline patient, focuses on the therapist's task of recognizing his participation as the recipient of the patient's projective identification, as well as on his efforts to make use of this awareness in determining the content and timing of his interventions.

> Mr. C., an unmarried 29-year-old man, had been in psychotherapy three times per week for about a month. At that time he was functioning well as a stockbroker, although he had had two psychotic episodes during college, both requiring brief hospitalizations.
>
> The patient had struggled for most of his life with feelings of "losing himself" in his father. The father would take intense interest in many of the patient's activities (Little League, science projects, homework, girlfriends, etc.) to the point that the patient lost the feeling of the activity being in any sense his own. For a period of four years following his second psychotic break, it had been necessary for Mr. C. to sever all ties with his father in order to maintain a sense of his own separate identity. The patient's mother was described in sparse detail and referred to simply as "a shadow" of her husband.
>
> At the beginning of the second month of therapy, a senior member of the brokerage house where the patient was working, a man who had been a mentor for the patient, rather suddenly left the firm to accept a position in another city. The patient began to fill each session with talk that sounded like free association, but had the effect of forcibly crowding the therapist out. Mr. C.'s speech was pressured and did not invite, or leave a moment's pause for, any kind of comment by the therapist. After several weeks the patient told the therapist that he had seen him on the street in front of his office talking with someone whom he believed to be a

colleague of the therapist. Mr. C. said that the therapist looked awkward, self-conscious, and weak. Mr. C. imagined that the colleague was more competent and successful than the therapist and that the therapist was getting advice of some sort from the colleague. The patient said he felt guilty for saying this to the therapist and did not want to hurt him, but that was the way he felt.

The therapist, although not usually rattled by insults from his patients, began to feel increasingly uneasy as time went on. He began to feel that his voice sounded thin when the patient allowed him an opportunity to speak. Mr. C. reported that he felt "very macho" during the sessions and felt guilty about the "fact" that he was more athletic and handsome than the therapist and could probably beat him at any sport. This denigration of the therapist as weak, unattractive, and emasculated continued over the succeeding weeks. These ideas were no longer labeled as feelings and came to be treated as objective facts. The subtle process of twisting reality was a more potent interpersonal force than the overt insults. The therapist was aware that feelings of weakness vis-à-vis his own father had been rekindled by this interaction with the patient. As the therapist experienced these feelings, he had the fantasy that the patient would eventually find him so ineffectual that he would leave in search of a new therapist. At this point the therapist attributed this fantasy to his conflicts related to his own father and explored with himself where things stood at present in that regard. The therapist decided not to intervene until he had a better grasp of the transference meaning of what was occurring.

About three months into the therapy, the therapist began to become aware of something that he had formerly only been preconsciously aware of: the patient had made no reference to his former mentor at work since he had initially spoken about the man's sudden departure. Mr. C. had not made a great deal of the event when first presenting it. However, as the therapist thought more about the changes that had taken place in the patient over the previous two months, and the powerful countertransference feelings of inadequacy and emasculation, he began to consider the possibility that his own feelings had been to a large extent evoked by the patient as a component of a projective identification that involved the patient's feelings of inadequacy in relation to a paternal transference figure. Although the details of this projective identification were still to be elucidated, the therapist found that the perspective of projective identification had already begun to release him from the previous countertransference pressure that he had been experiencing and allowed him to create psychological room within which he could now think about what was occurring in the transference.

It is apparent in the foregoing account that it was not possible for the therapist to comfortably observe the unfolding of the patient's conflicted paternal transference in the therapy, which was being expressed in part via a projection onto the mentor and in part through the transference. Instead, the therapist found himself in the midst of a stressful and confusing development wherein he felt intensely inadequate and ashamed of the sound of his own voice. When a therapist finds himself shaken in this way, he is very likely serving as the recipient of a projective identification. The therapist was aware that feelings of weakness had an important history in his own life and was able to consider the developments in his current life that might have contributed to an intensification of this conflict. However, the perspective of projective identification allowed the therapist to make use of his feeling-state to inform his understanding of the transference, and not simply to further his understanding of himself or to prevent his own conflicts from interfering with the therapy.

Once one has begun to formulate an interaction in terms of projective identification, it is often useful to refrain from interpreting or intervening until one has lived with the evoked feelings for some time. For example, the therapist did not attempt to alleviate the discomfort arising from feelings of inadequacy by immediately interpreting the hostility (which was clearly present) in the patient's denigrating comments about the therapist. It was only by containing these feelings *in the therapeutic situation* that the therapist was able to allow associative linkages to emerge in his own mind clearly enough to be recognized and thought about. Frequently, the psychological strain from the evoked feelings diminishes and the therapist is able to gain psychological distance when these feelings are recognized as components of a projective identification.

Before this distance has been achieved, however, the therapist's interventions are likely to be motivated by conscious and unconscious efforts to get the patient to stop doing whatever it is that he is doing that is leading to the therapist's feelings of being controlled or attacked or strangulated or imprisoned or paralyzed. These countertransference feelings represent only a few of the more common unconscious fantasies evoked in the therapist while he is serving as the recipient of a projective identification. (See chapters 7 and 8 for further clinical material illustrating the way in which the therapist's wishes to be released from an intense form of interpersonal pressure are balanced against the therapist's efforts to refrain from intervening until he feels he is doing so from a position of sufficient psychological distance.)

INTERPRETATION OF PROJECTIVE IDENTIFICATION

Mr. C.'s psychotherapy illustrates certain technical principles that come into play once the therapist has successfully begun to formulate an interaction in terms of projective identification.

When the therapist felt he understood at least one level of the patient's current defensive activity, he commented that Mr. C. had said very little about his mentor, Mr. J., and that this had been particularly true since Mr. J. had left the firm. The patient described how Mr. J. had taken great interest in him and at one point had sided with the patient on a major protocol dispute at considerable risk to his own position in the firm. Mr. C. felt that Mr. J. had been able to see something in him that no one else had been able to recognize. The patient added that he had hardly noticed Mr. J.'s absence and that a colleague at work had accurately pointed out that Mr. J. had had more charm than brains.

Mr. C. then returned to talking in a pressured, hypermasculine way with continued indirect reference to the now-accepted perception of the therapist as weak and inadequate. It was becoming clear to the therapist that the patient was having great difficulty accepting the loss of Mr. J. and that projective identification involving fantasied extrusion of the weak and abandoned self was being used in part as a defense against feelings of loss and disappointment.

The therapist listened for several more sessions in order to be sure that subsequent material supported this hypothesis. The therapist then made use of one of many available opportunities to comment on the way in which the patient had accepted as fact the therapist's physical and professional inadequacy. Mr. C. was at first somewhat surprised to have such a basic aspect of reality called into question. As he thought further about it, though, he was somewhat surprised by the way he had been thinking and acting. He reiterated that during the past weeks he had been feeling "very macho," and that it had felt so good to feel that way that he hated to talk about the subject because it might interfere with that feeling.

The therapist said that he thought that when Mr. J. left the agency, the patient had felt as if a valuable part of himself had been lost, the part that only Mr. J. had been able to appreciate. The patient confirmed this and said that he had felt empty in a very literal way. He said that when he heard the news, the first thing he did was to go to the candy machine in the basement of the building and buy several candy bars and eat them "almost in one mouthful." He said that, oddly enough, this failed to make him feel full, but he had decided not to eat any more because he began to feel nauseated. Later in the session the therapist said that he thought that Mr. C. now felt left with the dregs of himself and was trying to rid himself of these feelings by viewing the therapist as the weak, ineffectual person that the patient now felt himself to be. Mr. C. said that he felt embarrassed to say this because it sounded so childish, but he had wished to be Mr. J.'s son and that he had frequently daydreamed about being a member of his family. For the first time in two months there were reflective silences in the session.

During the succeeding session, the patient reported a dream. In that dream Mr. C. was in a barbershop having his hair cut when suddenly he noticed that too much had been taken off, and he sobbed as he stared at the hair on the floor. Mr. C. associated the hair with Mr. J.'s greying hair. This had been of concern to the patient, since it reflected Mr. J.'s age and the danger of his dying. Also the hair was associated with the story of Samson, "who lost his strength when his hair was cut off." The relation of the dream to the projective identification that had been interpreted was clear to the patient: in fantasy, a part of himself that was mixed up with Mr. J. had been lost and only now was the sadness being felt. (Hair is a particularly apt symbol, in that it is simultaneously a part of self and not-self. This ambiguity was utilized in the dream to express a similar relation to Mr. J. and to the therapist.) Clearly, still another level of the dream involved the idea of having been emasculated by castration as represented by the haircut, the Samson legend, and so forth. This level of meaning bore directly on the feeling of emasculation evoked in the therapist in the course of the projective identification under discussion.

The therapist had laid the groundwork for an interpretation of the projective identification by calling into question the "fact" of the therapist's weakness. Without this initial differentiation of the fantasy component of projective identification from reality, the patient's understanding of the interaction would probably not have been possible. As long as the therapist *is* the weak self, the patient cannot consider the way in which the *idea* of the weak therapist serves as a defense against feelings of inadequacy. The distortion of a specific aspect of reality is an important interpersonal means by which pressure is exerted on the object to see himself in a way that conforms with the patient's unconscious projective fantasy. Focusing upon this alteration of reality is often a crucial preparatory step for the interpretation of a projective identification.

The interpretation that was eventually offered involved explicit reference to: the patient's unconscious conception of a loss of a valued part of himself that had resulted from Mr. J.'s departure; the defensive fantasy of locating the weak self in the therapist; and the reality of the interpersonal interaction by means of which these fantasies were enacted.

The patient's enhanced capacity to experience feelings of loss as represented in the dream served as a partial validation for the interpretation. Equally important was the change in the relationship to the therapist that followed the intervention. The patient's increased capacity to tolerate thoughtful silences afforded the therapist the opportunity to formulate his own thoughts and to intervene at times. It meant that the therapist no longer had to be so tightly controlled and so urgently kept at arm's length by means of the patient's verbal flooding of the sessions. The projective identification described served as a defense not only against feelings of loss in relation to Mr. J., but also (and perhaps even more difficult for the patient) the anxiety of beginning therapy. He was particularly fearful of a type of involvement with the therapist that could potentially lead to painful and conflicted paternal transferences, including feelings of melting into the father and intense castration anxiety.

This vignette illustrates a technical approach that is suited to patients who are capable of a relatively high level of self–object differentiation at the same time as, or shortly after, they experience feelings and fantasies that reflect blurred self–object boundaries. In other words, patients like the one described, either as a result of preexisting strengths or of previous work in psychotherapy, are able to think in a differentiated way about experience involving poor self–object differentiation. As will be seen in chapters 7 and 8, schizophrenic and severely borderline patients are often incapable of such mental functioning, and one's techniques must be modified in the direction "silent interpretations" until an adequate capacity for symbolization and self–object differentiation has been developed.

TECHNICAL PROBLEMS OF CONTAINMENT

I would now like to focus on the psychological work involved in serving therapeutically as a recipient of the patient's projective identifications. Processing the projective identification without acting upon the engendered feelings is an essential aspect of the therapeutic process (Heimann, 1950; Malin & Grotstein, 1966). Acceptance of the projected aspects of the patient as a communication to be understood—as opposed to proddings or assaults to be acted upon or fled from—constitutes the background of the therapeutic situation. The importance of an accepting therapeutic environment cannot be overemphasized. When the containment process fails, the therapist forces back into the patient those aspects of self that the patient was attempting to project into the therapist. In such cases, the therapist's interventions overtly or covertly state: "You're trying to make me feel your pain (or experience your insanity) for you." Of course, this is one aspect of all projective identifications, but if this aspect alone is addressed, the patient will simply feel chastised for attempting to do something selfish and destructive.

Establishing in a given situation what it means to "live with" the feelings engendered in the course of projective identification can be a complex task. As will be seen in the following vignette, the idea of containment can become distorted at times, serving as a rationalization for "therapeutic" masochism.

> Dr. S., a European psychiatrist in her late forties who had worked extensively with young adults on an outpatient basis, began working on a long-term adolescent inpatient service staffed almost exclusively by psychiatrists and nurses in their late twenties and early thirties. Not long after Dr. S. joined the staff of this ward, a number of patients began using her in the service of splitting, i.e., villainized her and contrasted her with the "good" staff members. She also served as an object of projective identification in such a way that she was relentlessly treated by the patients (and to a much lesser extent by portions of the staff) as an object of derision and contempt. Dr. S. had read about projective identification and felt that it was her job to serve as a container for the bitter, negative maternal-transference feelings that she recognized as a basic component of the behavior of the patients. Within a few months, the job became so painful and undermining of her self-esteem that Dr. S. did not know how she could continue to work on the ward. Before finalizing her plans to transfer to another section of the department, she sought consultation with an outside psychiatrist in an effort to determine whether she was unconsciously contributing to or perpetuating the painful situation.
>
> In the course of the consultation, Dr. S. talked about feeling like a failure for not being able to "take it" from the patients. She knew from experience that working with adolescents was difficult, but she felt totally demoralized by their manner of looking through her and treating her as if the idea of being in the same room with her were repugnant. She talked about her wish to demonstrate to herself that she

could contain their bitterness and disdain, which she understood in terms of splitting and projective identification.

Despite the accuracy of her understanding of the transference meaning of the patients' contempt, Dr. S. was not fully aware of the way she had masochistically interpreted her own role as "container" for these feelings. She was confusing the active psychological work of processing feelings evoked in the course of projective identification with the act of endlessly enduring punishment. As a result, Dr. S. had failed to integrate the induced feelings with other aspects of her personality. If such integration had taken place, she might have been able to mobilize more reality-based self- and object-representations, which would have included views of herself as a highly skilled clinician who had chosen to make herself available to this particular group of patients for the purpose of engaging in psychological work. This does not constitute a blank check for the exercise of the patients' sadism. Simple enactment of anger and contempt can be done anywhere and does not require the services of a therapist or a psychiatric hospital staff. Since Dr. S. had not felt able to reassert the reality of the therapeutic context for her interactions with the patients, she raised the matter in clinical meetings of the ward's staff.

Dr. S.'s previous self-understanding gained in her personal analysis made it possible for her in the course of the consultation to recognize and loosen her hold upon long-standing unconscious wishes to serve as a martyr in a parent–child relationship. She raised her concerns in clinical meetings with fellow staff members, and these discussions led to a rectification of the therapeutic framework. Dr. S. began to see and present herself as a member of the ward staff and not as an appendage to it. Her feelings of discomfort were now discussed by her at ward meetings as data emanating from a therapeutic interaction and not as admissions of failure.

It is essential that inpatient psychiatric services conduct clinical meetings in such a way that issues of this type can be discussed without fear of further attack by fellow staff members. When the leadership of a ward fails to provide a safe forum of this type, staff members are forced to attempt to manage emotional strain in isolation. In my experience, this results in a virtual shutdown of therapeutic work on the ward (even in individual psychotherapy), since staff members are no longer able to risk making themselves sufficiently emotionally available (and vulnerable) to deal with feelings that inevitably arise in the course of genuine therapeutic work.

In the above discussion, the focus was on the masochistic misuse of the concept of containment. A related problem regularly arises in the psychotherapy of potentially violent or suicidal patients. With such patients there is often intense pressure on a therapist to allow the patient to dictate the terms of the therapeutic relationship. The following material from the treatment of a suicidal patient highlights the special difficulties entailed in the containment process when there is a self-destructive threat looming over the therapeutic work. The clinical data are from a consultation involving a therapist who had reached an impasse in his work with a chronically suicidal, intermittently psychotic patient whom he had been seeing three times a week for two years.

> The therapist sought consultation because he felt physically assaulted ("like I was getting punched in the stomach") by the patient's intense dependency and the constant threat of suicide, both of which had reached a crescendo after about a year of therapy. The patient, Mrs. N., had been depressed but not suicidal until shortly before the therapist's vacation during the 11th month of therapy. Shortly after the therapist returned, the patient took a moderately serious overdose of antidepressant medication and then called the therapist, who arranged for emergency treatment at a crisis

clinic. Mrs. N., now 28 years old, had made a serious suicide attempt in her early twenties and had been hospitalized at that time. She told the therapist that during her hospitalization eight years earlier, she had been unfairly held in the hospital on an involuntary committment order. She was adamant that she would never consent to hospitalization again.

The therapist retrospectively viewed the patient's overdose as marking a turning point in the treatment. He felt that at that point he had been forced to either discontinue treatment or treat Mrs. N. as an outpatient, knowing that he had to be prepared to accept the considerable risk of her suicide. He had decided on the latter course. In the consultation, the therapist reported that over the past several months the patient had looked increasingly pale and wasted, "like a dying patient." She would report "howling in pain like an animal" for hours at a time in her room. For months the therapist had expected that each phone call he received would bring news of Mrs. N.'s suicide. More recently, he had become aware of intense wishes that she would die and get it over with.

The patient was the eldest of three children. Her father was an alcoholic, and her mother a chronically depressed woman who spent large parts of each day alone in her room crying. There was such difficulty in getting the mother's attention that the patient would write notes to her in the hope of eventually having her mother read them.

Mrs. N. remembers that when she was 10 years old her mother came into her room in the middle of the night to give her a kiss, which the patient refused by turning away. The next thing the patient recalls is hearing a loud blast from the next room. Her mother had shot herself in the head. Mrs. N. reports that she was told at the funeral not to upset her younger brothers by crying, and also that she was the one who caused the suicide.

The therapist indicated that in the week prior to the

consultation he had said something to the patient that had made him feel better, but he did not know if it had done the patient any good. He had told her that it was impossible for him to think clearly and work effectively with her as long as suicide was a constant and immediate threat, as it had been for the past year. He went on to say to her that he knew that she was terribly depressed, but somehow the threat of suicide had to be put on the back burner.

The consultant pointed out that even though the therapist had not been thinking in terms of projective identification, his intervention concerning his unwillingness to accept the threat of suicide as the constant background for the therapy represented a clear statement of the successful elements of his own containment of a projective identification. The problem was that the therapist, not having the perspective of projective identification in mind, had been unable to formulate for himself the rationale for his intervention and consequently did not know how to follow up.

From the perspective of the concept of projective identification, the second year of the therapy could be seen as an interpersonal enactment of a specific internal object relationship, wherein the therapist was being forced to experience the unbearable responsibility felt by a 10-year-old girl for the life and death of her depressed, chronically suicidal mother. Mrs. N. could tolerate neither the continual dread of her mother's suicide (now an internalized mother representation) nor her hatred of and murderous wishes toward her mother for being so depressed and distant.

The therapist's intervention pointed out that an identical burden of responsibility for the life of a suicidally depressed woman was being forced upon him. Moreover, he was implying that, unlike the patient, he did not feel limited to the range of emotions and alternatives that the patient had had available to her at age 10 in her relationship with her mother. The therapist was implicitly stating that, despite the feelings of responsibility engendered in him, in reality he was not a 10-year-old girl with a depressed mother; he was a therapist with a depressed patient, and there is a world of difference between the two. The feeling of relief that the therapist had experienced after making this intervention reflected the fact that he had begun to free himself from the unconscious feeling that there was no choice but to play a specific role in the patient's unconscious fantasy. However, the therapist was in danger of simply forcing back into the patient that aspect of herself (the little girl with the hated responsibility for her mother) which she was attempting to communicate to the therapist by means of projective identification.

What was missing in the intervention was the therapist's statement of understanding of Mrs. N.'s unconscious reasons for feeling and behaving as she was toward the therapist. As with all interpretations, the therapist should begin with whatever the patient can accept and over time, following the lead of the patient, gradually address the more disowned and threatening material. In interpreting projective identifications, it is important to acknowledge the patient's attempt to communicate something important about himself rather than simply addressing the hostile, controlling, and escapist motivations which are almost always present as elements of projective identification. These latter motivations are usually far more unacceptable to the patient than his wish to communicate and, if prematurely interpreted, will be heard as accusatory and strenuously warded off.

The consultant suggested that the therapist's intervention might be supplementd by an interpretation of the following type: "I think you'd like me to know what it was like to feel fully responsible for your mother and yet totally unable to help her." If the clinical material that followed validated this partial interpretation, then over time, as the opportunity arose, it would be important to address the patient's unconscious fantasy of turning the therapist into the helpless 10-year-old girl that the patient still felt herself to be. In the course of the analysis of this unconscious projective fantasy, the therapist would be likely to encounter the full intensity of the patient's transference hatred of the mother-therapist, as well as the omnipotent wish to eject painful aspects of herself and her internalized objects while simultaneously maintaining the internalized object relationship (the tie to the depressed mother).

The therapist viewed succeeding sessions with the consultant's comments in mind and confirmed for himself that the therapy had in an important sense become an enactment of an internal drama, in which he had become limited to playing the role of the patient as a 10-year-old girl vis-à-vis her suicidal mother. The interpretation of the transference (in this case, a projective identification) was initiated along the lines discussed above.

As this work was being done, Mrs. N. began to talk in therapy more than previously, reported a dream (which was an unusual event in this therapy), and noticed similarities between the way she was treating her daughter and the way she felt her mother had treated her. There was a marked diminution of suicidal threats with an accompanying reduction of pressure on the therapist to continually imagine himself receiving news of the patient's suicide.

Over the next several months, the therapist noted that the patient seemed sexually attractive to him for the first time. The patient had made only fleeting references to sex during the first two years of the therapy but now began to complain that she hated the way her husband acted as if sex with her were his right. A new level of transference and countertransference was now unfolding that had been defended against by means of the projective identification (a transference resistance) described above.

ENACTMENT OF THE CONTAINMENT PROCESS

There are times when the therapist finds that his interpretations are treated as dangerous and unassimilable by the patient. In this section, material will be presented that reflects a very common clinical situation in work with borderline and schizophrenic patients who are unable to make use of verbal interpretation because of their fear of being taken over by the therapist. Under such circumstances, the therapist must find other ways of talking with the patient until the patient's experience in the therapy has rendered these fears manageable.

> A 22-year-old chronic schizophrenic patient, Mr. G., had been in psychotherapy four times per week for three years when he entered a period of acute psychotic decompensation. This breakdown marked the end of three years of rather sustained progress from his initial delusional, disoriented, intermittently mute, and immobile state that had led to the seven-month hospitalization during which therapy was begun. Over the course of the psychotherapy, Mr. G. had gradually achieved a successful adaption to a halfway house and junior college which represented the highest level of functioning he had attained in his life.
>
> Principal themes in the therapy were Mr. G.'s insistence that he did not have the slightest interest in therapy or growth or change of any type, and that he had many secrets, none of which were ever to be revealed to the therapist. The interaction in the therapy characteristically took the form of the patient's being silent for most of the session and occasionally volunteering vague, fragmentary information that demanded follow-up questions from the therapist. Mr. G. would respond to requests for clarification or interpretation with equally evasive comments which invited further questions. These incomplete thoughts and partially answered questions served to establish a connection with the therapist

while at the same time confirming for the patient that he still had possession of his secrets. These secrets were the patient's assurance that the therapist did not fully know him, and therefore that he still had an existence separate from the therapist.

Mr. G. felt that the progress he had made in psychological and social functioning was disturbing evidence that he was literally becoming the therapist. In the psychotic decompensation at the beginning of the fourth year of work, the patient lay motionless in bed for most of the day and referred to himself by a name that was a condensation of the therapist's street address and last name. The psychotic symptomatology (paranoid delusions, hallucinations, fragmented thoughts, loss of sense of self) steadily diminished over a two-month period. However, after the resolution of the acute regression, Mr. G. did not regain his previous level of verbal or social functioning and would stay in bed whenever permitted to do so. His personal hygiene had deteriorated to the point that he looked and smelled like a derelict. His face and hands were dark with dirt and his clothes were covered with food stains. For the first time in the therapy, many appointments were missed, sometimes as many as three of his four weekly sessions. By about eight weeks after the onset of the acute decompensation, his "regressed" behavior had changed to a form of stubborn defiance that was to a considerable degree under his conscious control. The therapist interpreted to the patient that he felt that Mr. G. was afraid that continued progress would mean he would become increasingly like the therapist, finally turning into the therapist, and thereby losing himself as a separate person. Over the succeeding four months, Mr. G.'s attendance became even more erratic, virtually bringing the therapy to an end. The therapy seemed to exist in spite of the patient.

The therapist experienced such feelings of frustration, defeat, and denigration in his work with the patient that he frequently looked forward to the complete discontinuation of the therapy. These feelings were experienced concurrently with the fantasy that liberation from Mr. G. as a result of the cessation of therapy would be won at tremendous cost to the therapist's reputation and professional self-regard, both of which were now felt to stem from the successful treatment of "patients like this one."

During this period, the therapist became increasingly cognizant of the fact that he felt impossibly trapped by this patient. He recognized that he had been induced to feel not only disproportionately responsible for maintaining the therapy (the linkage to the patient) but also dependent upon the therapy as a source of self-esteem. At the same time Mr. G., through his relentless treatment-attacking behavior, had led the therapist to experience an intense wish for a complete disruption of the relationship (Altshul, 1980). It had not proved possible to influence the stalemate by means of interpretation. In fact, interpretation seemed to add fuel to the fire, because the very act of attempting to understand meanings was seen by the patient as the essence of the therapist and therefore had to be strenuously warded off.

After reflecting upon this for some time, the therapist decided to desist from further interpretation and attempted to find a way of offering the patient something that would bear the patient's own mark, not that of the therapist. The therapist said to Mr. G. that it did not seem fair that Mr. G. should be the only one able to enjoy the pleasure and security of knowing that things would never change. The therapist indicated that he too was now ready not only to accept but to savor the knowledge that during the time he spent with the patient (which he hoped would be the rest of his life) nothing would ever change. There would be no surprises, no unearthed secrets, and no revelations. The remainder of that hour was spent in silence.

Mr. G. was early for the following session, which was the first time in over two months that he had attended two consecutive meetings. After about 20 minutes of silence, he asked, "Are we going to play stubborn again today?" The therapist silently noted the patient's perception of the element of play in the current interaction. He responded to the patient's question by saying that the answer to that question was a secret. The patient smiled. After being asked another question, the therapist said, "What if I need all of my secrets and feel that each time I answer a question, I give something of myself to you and therefore lose a part of myself? What if I feel that if I were to go on giving away secrets, I'd eventually have nothing left of myself and would disappear?" The patient laughed deeply at this.

Over the next months, this form of play continued, with the therapist insisting on his need to keep things exactly as they were. Mr. G. pointed out the hostility in this secretiveness, as well as the pleasure the therapist seemed to derive from excluding the patient from his secrets. Mr. G. later observed that the therapist's stubbornness had the effect of "luring me in up to a point and then slamming the door on me." After three more weeks, the patient brought in an application to reenter college that required the therapist's signature, since a medical leave had been taken. The therapist said, "As you know, I hate change of any kind, but if you insist on spending your time at school, I might as well sign the form."

The interaction characterizing this phase of therapy represented a playful enactment of the therapist's containment of irreconcilable elements of the patient that had been induced in the therapist as a part of a projective identification. The therapist was being asked/forced to contain the fear of merger and the wish for connectedness, the fear of utter disconnectedness and the wish for separateness. The therapist playfully mirrored the patient's need for separateness as well as the conflicting need for relatedness.

What the therapist added was an integrated version of these

irreconcilable elements: the therapist enacted an image of himself and the patient, forever secretive and yet forever accepting of that secretiveness, so that disconnectedness need never be imposed as a remedy. Identification with the therapist had formerly been experienced as a threat to the patient's separate existence. The therapist's unanxious mirroring presented to the patient a form of identification that was well regulated and even pleasurable and did not threaten the therapist's sense of self. The therapist's playful containment of the patient's projective identification provided the patient with a modification of that which the patient recognized as himself and therefore did not have to fend off for fear of being taken over by the therapist.

Ordinarily, using words to interpret what is occurring between the patient and therapist is the most economical, direct, and precise way of communicating with a patient. When interpretations are treated by the patient as dangerous and unassimilable threats to the integrity of his sense of self, the therapist must find other ways of communicating with the patient in order to facilitate the process of reintegration of the patient's projections.

WORK WITH PROFOUNDLY REGRESSED PATIENTS

In periods of profound regression schizophrenic patients are not capable of sustaining even the most rudimentary form of fantasy activity and thus are incapable of sustained projective identifications, which necessarily involve unconscious projective fantasies. When these patients do begin to evidence projective identification, it is of a very primitive type, based on sensory-level precursors of what will later become visually and verbally symbolized fantasy activity.

The "fantasies" of evacuation underlying the earliest forms

of projective identification are little more than preverbal proprioceptive, visceral, muscular, and to some extent visual representations of expulsion of inner contents into a receptacle that is vaguely felt to be human and dimly recognized as non-self. (For example, one schizophrenic patient enacted a rudimentary fantasy of dumping lifeless mental contents into the therapist by each session talking incoherently while picking at the keratinized skin on the bottoms of her feet and letting the flakes of debris pile up on the carpet below.) Very gradually, the fantasy underlying projective identification becomes reworked into forms that are increasingly specific and differentiated, as the patient's mode of symbolization becomes predominantly visual and verbal. Such reworking of unconscious fantasy in the course of therapy leads to an increase in the clarity and definition of the aspect of self that is unconsciously ejected by the patient and evoked in the therapist in the course of projective identification.

In early phases of work with chronic schizophrenic patients, interpretations are developed verbally in the therapist's mind but not presented to the patient. These early formulations, or silent interpretations, represent a part of an internal dialogue in which the therapist is attempting to make sense for himself of what is being dumped into him. The therapist makes available to the patient his understanding of the impressions that have piled up in him as much through the rhythm and tone of his voice as through the content of what he says; as much by his facial expression and muscle tension as through the facet of the interaction that the therapist chooses to focus upon; as much by the way he looks at the patient who is grimacing bizarrely as through what he says to the patient about it.

The deeply regressed patient's disorganized thoughts and feelings (or their precursors) are often experienced by the patient as meaningless stimulation. When the patient is capable of primitive forms of projective identification, he will attempt to dump his meaningless mental contents into the therapist, partly in an effort to gain help in organizing his chaotic internal world. The therapist's function of rendering meaningful that which is meaningless to the patient is analogous to the function served by the mother when she responds to her infant's "needs" before he has any notion of what his needs are. Her responsive caretaking gives meaning and definition to what had formerly been simply a barrage of stimulation. The infant's diffuse, unlocalized distress (not even experienced as a feeling) gradually becomes a feeling of hunger as that distress is linked (by means of the mother's response to it) to the experience of sucking, swallowing, tasting, abdominal fullness, being held in a particular way, and so forth. Just as the mother conveys to the infant the meaning of his experience through her handling of the infant, the therapist of the severely ill schizophrenic patient renders meaningful and manageable what had existed in the patient's mind as chaotic precursors of discrete thoughts and feelings. Only when the patient is able to use verbal symbolism, as opposed to symbolic equation in the formation of projective identifications, does verbal interpretation of the underlying fantasy content become possible and useful.[3]

TRANSFERENCE, COUNTERTRANSFERENCE, AND PROJECTIVE IDENTIFICATION

Questions about the relationship of transference and countertransference to projective identification have undoubtedly arisen in the course of this chapter. For example, what is the

---

[3]In her classic paper on symbol formation, Segal (1957) defines *symbolic equation* as that mode of symbol formation wherein the symbol and the symbolized are treated as identical. For example, a schizophrenic patient who was no longer able to play a violin in front of an audience explained that it would be unthinkable to masturbate in public. The symbolic meaning of violin playing (masturbation) was treated as identical to the act of masturbation itself. In contrast, mature symbol formation involves an ego capable of viewing the symbol as a creation that *represents* the symbolized but is not equivalent to it.

difference between transference and projective identification? Aren't transference interpretations focused on precisely the same juxtaposition of internal and external reality as interpretations of projective identification? This similarity between the interpretation of projective identification and the interpretation of transference does in fact exist because *projective identification represents an aspect of transference.* Projective identification is that aspect of transference that involves the therapist's being enlisted in an interpersonal actualization (an actual enactment between patient and therapist) of a segment of the patient's internal object world.[4]

Some forms of transference involve very little interpersonal actualization; that is, they do not require the same degree of feeling-participation (Searles, 1963) on the part of the therapist. For example, in the therapy of relatively well functioning neurotic patients, there is frequently minimal pressure on the therapist to participate in an interpersonal enactment of the transference and correspondingly little evidence of either incomplete differentiation of self and object or unconscious wishes to control and influence the therapist from within. Under such circumstances, the therapist's relationship to the patient's experience is an empathic one. Using Schafer's (1959) definition, empathy consists of "sharing in" and cognitively and affectively understanding the psychological state of another person, who is recognized and experienced as a whole and separate person at a particular juncture in his life. In a therapeutic interaction characterized by projective identification, the term *empathy* aptly describes the successful outcome of the therapist's active psychological work of containment.

This leads us to a related question: Is projective identification an aspect of transference that is encountered only in work with psychotic patients? In thinking about this question, it is important to keep in mind that in the course of psychological

[4]Elements of transference that lie outside the realms of unconscious fantasy and interpersonal relations (and therefore beyond projective identification) will be discussed in chapter 8.

development, modes of functioning characteristic of earlier stages persist in later stages of development (Freud, 1905). These earlier modes continue as strata of more advanced modes of functioning. Under circumstances such as a therapeutic regression, the earlier components may become predominant for a period of time (for example, in a given transference reenactment).

Freud (1905) demonstrated that oral, anal, and phallic phases of infantile sexuality not only serve as precursors of mature genital sexuality but also persist in a relatively unchanged form (for example, in foreplay) even in mature sexuality. Similarly, in the development of object relations, primitive nonverbal modes of relatedness persist as the coenesthetic background for diacritic modes of interpersonal communication.[5] In other words, alongside the specificity of communication that is possible with verbal symbols, less well defined and often contradictory sets of unconscious thoughts and feelings are communicated through the look in one's eye, the tension in one's forehead, the timbre of one's voice, and so forth. Without the nuances and ambiguities provided by these earlier modes of communication, mature relatedness would be stark and machinelike.

Projective identification is one of the earliest forms of linkage between mother and infant wherein initially the mother serves as the container for elements of the infant's perceptions and responds to the infant in a way that endows his sensory state with meaning. Later, the infant internalizes aspects of the mother's personality structure by introjecting aspects of her unconscious projections, that is, by functioning as the recipient of her projective identifications.

In the course of development, projective identification recedes into the background as it is superseded by verbally sym-

---

[5]Spitz (1945, 1965) used the term *coenesthetic* to refer to visceral modes of perception and expression based in the autonomic nervous system. Later in development, the infant develops *diacritic* modes that are organized in the cerebral cortex and are reflected in the specificity and definition that characterize higher-level cognitive processes and conscious thought.

bolized communication in conjunction with modes of relatedness based on well-differentiated self- and object-representations. However, even in mature forms of object relations, projective identification continues as an unconscious substratum that unobtrusively complements the mature modes of functioning which predominate. There is always an unconscious demand and expectation that the other person know precisely what one is feeling. We never entirely make our peace with the reality that we are alone with our thoughts and feelings and that others can only know an inexact approximation of our internal state.

Projective identification represents a component of all adult object relations, including the way in which the well-integrated analysand relates to his analyst and the way his analyst relates to him. Those who view projective identification as "a basically psychotic mechanism" (Meissner, 1980) confuse that which is primitive with that which is psychotic. Diffusion of ego boundaries and treatment of the object as an extension of the self are characteristics of psychotic states, but they also have their place in a hierarchy of modes of relatedness that constitute the healthy personality. Controlled access in therapy to more primitive modes of relatedness, including transferences in the form of projective identification, is a mark of the well-functioning personality.

If projective identification is to be considered an aspect of transference, what then is the relationship between this type of transference and the countertransference? Many analysts (Greenson, 1967; Reich, 1951, 1960, 1966) limit the concept of countertransference to those responses of the therapist that stem from his own needs and conflicts. It is indeed essential that the therapist attempt to separate those responses to the patient that reflect his own wishes, fears, and conflicts and those that reflect mature reactions to the realistically perceived current interaction. Although this type of categorization constitutes a necessary aspect of countertransference analysis, it has not seemed to me to be the most useful way of organizing and understanding the therapist's responses to the patient. All of the therapist's feelings will be overdetermined combinations of mature, reality-based responses and irrational transferences. The feelings experienced by the therapist in relation to the patient "come to him, like all feelings, without tags showing whence they have come" (Searles, 1959, p. 300). Therefore, I find it useful to include in the concept of countertransference all of the therapist's responses to the patient and to the therapeutic situation.

Within the totality of the therapist's response to the patient, there are two components that are of central therapeutic concern inasmuch as they bear directly on the way in which the therapist learns about the patient's unconscious internal world. These are (1) the therapist's identification with the patient's unconscious experience of self in the internal object relationship that is being played out in the transference ("concordant indentification," Racker, 1957) and (2) the therapist's identification with the object component of the patient's internal object relationship that underlies the transference ("complementary identification," Racker, 1957).

These two types of identification are the means by which the projected aspect of the person projectively identifying is "taken in" by the recipient. Hence, just as projective identification can be understood as an aspect of transference, the recipient's response to the projective identification constitutes an aspect of countertransference. This potential for the linkage of transference and countertransference experience accounts for the special place of the concept of projective identification in psychoanalytic theory.

Countertransference analysis is the means by which the therapist attempts to understand and make therapeutic use of his response to the patient. This is not an effort to "get through," "filter out," or "overcome" what the therapist recognizes as a reflection of his own personality; rather, the therapist makes use of his self-understanding to determine how his feelings and thoughts have been uniquely shaped and colored by his present experience with this patient at this point in the therapy, and in particular by the specific qualities of the patient's predominant transferences to the therapist.

What has been said should not be mistaken as a proposal that all of the therapist's feelings should be treated as if they bore a one-to-one correspondence to an aspect of the patient's experience. This is clearly not the case. However, what the therapist is experiencing, even if it is a set of feelings recognized as having meanings determined by the therapist's internalized past experience, is at the same time a response to something that has occurred *in this hour with this patient.* Something that we have come to understand about our patients also holds true for therapists: people do not project into a vacuum—there is always a kernel of reality onto which fantasies are hung. It is that kernel of the patient's internal psychic reality to which the therapist hopes to gain access by means of his analysis of the countertransference, even when those feelings are recognized predominantly as his own transferences to the patient.

SUMMARY

From the perspective of projective identification, the therapeutic process is understood as involving the patient who both entrusts with the therapist and forces upon the therapist an aspect of himself that he has been unable to integrate or make use of for the purpose of psychological growth. The role of the therapist is to make available to the patient for reinternalization that which was the patient's to begin with, now slightly modified as a result of having "reposed" (Bion, 1967) in the therapist.

When the therapist suspects that he has developed an intensely held, but highly limited view of himself and the patient that is in an important sense shared by the patient, he is very likely serving as an object of the patient's projective identification. In psychotherapeutic work with patients evidencing whole-object-related forms of transference, verbal interpretation frequently facilitates the patient's reinternalization of the slightly altered version of the aspect of himself that has been externalized by means of projective identification.

Interpretive work of this type includes an examination of one or more of the following aspects of the projective identification: (1) the specific distortions of reality introduced by the patient that serve as the interpersonal means by which the object is "instructed" about his role in the patient's unconscious projective fantasy; (2) the nature of the unconscious fantasy; (3) the defensive, expressive, object-seeking, and growth-seeking motivations for the interpersonal enactment of the projective fantasy; (4) the genetic context for the development of the projective identification; and (5) the role of the projective identification in maintaining the patient's current internal psychological equilibrium and system of object relations.

Patients who are evidencing almost entirely preverbal, part-object-related forms of transference often experience verbal interpretation as so foreign to their experience of themselves that interventions in that form can be internalized by the patient only at the cost of feeling that they have lost themselves in the therapist's words and ideas. Under such circumstances, the therapist must rely on noninterpretive interventions and management of the therapy to convey his silently formulated understandings of that which the patient has unconsciously asked him to both contain and return to him in a form that he can utilize.

4
CONTRASTING PSYCHOANALYTIC APPROACHES

Until recently very few therapists or analysts outside of the Kleinian group have used either the term or the concept of projective identification in their clinical thinking. However, inasmuch as the phenomena addressed by this concept (unconscious projective fantasies in interplay with congruent feelings evoked in the recipient) are an aspect of all psychotherapeutic work, each school of psychoanalytic thought has, over time, developed methods of handling this facet of the therapeutic interaction. In the present chapter, the relationship between the technical approach presented in this volume (see in particular chapters 2 and 3) and the principles of technique espoused by analysts of the classical, Kleinian, British Middle, and Modern Psychoanalytic Groups will be discussed.

THE KLEINIAN APPROACH

Because projective identification was first described by Melanie Klein (1946), it is commonly, though erroneously, assumed that it is inextricably linked with Kleinian theory (see, for example, Meissner, 1980).[1] Projective identification has no inherent connection with any aspect of specifically Kleinian metapsychology or clinical theory (for example, the Kleinian notion of the primacy of the death instinct, its assumptions concerning the infant's capacity for fantasy activity from the earliest days and weeks of life, and the idea that the Oedipus complex and superego develop in the first year of life).

Similarly, it is often incorrectly assumed that there is a necessary link between the clinical application of the concept of projective identification and Kleinian technique. In Kleinian technique (Klein, 1948, 1961; Segal, 1964, 1967), almost all interventions are made in the form of the interpretation of the unconscious fantasy underlying the principal anxiety of the session. In contrast with classical technique, these interpretations do not begin by addressing the more conscious and preconscious defensive aspects of the material. Instead, the content of the underlying unconscious fantasy is interpreted directly, the rationale being that it is these unconscious fantasies that are producing the central anxiety of the session and that the analyst would be remiss not to talk with the patient about what is bothering him (Klein, 1948). Moreover, these interpretations of unconscious fantasy (psychological manifestations of instinctual drives and defenses against these drive derivatives) are almost always transference interpretations and are offered from the very outset of therapy: "In my own experience I have not had a case in which I did not interpret the transference from the start" (Segal, 1967, p. 174).

What gives the Kleinian mode of handling projective identification its distinctive mark is the fact that for the Kleinians, the therapist's communication of his understanding of what has been projected into him is done almost exclusively in the form of verbalized transference interpretations. One of the problems

---

[1]A partial listing of analysts who have contributed to the development of Kleinian theory and technique includes Bion, Grinberg, Grotstein, Heimann, Isaacs, Mason, Meltzer, Milner, Money-Kyrle, Racker, Rey, Rivière, Rosenfeld, Segal, and Thorner.

with this is that a patient's reliance upon projective identification as a predominant mode of communication, defense, and object-relatedness is frequently a reflection of the fact that he is currently unable to make use of verbal symbols either intrapsychically (as a part of an internal dialogue) or interpersonally. As a result, he can neither comprehend nor utilize interpretations offered in a verbalized form.

When the therapist relies entirely on verbal interpretations to deal with preverbal phenomena, one of the following outcomes often develops: (1) the relatively healthy patient may attempt to accommodate by translating his preverbal experience in the transference into the terms of a phase of development in which experience was verbally symbolized (for example, the Oedipal level of development); (2) the more disturbed patient will frequently experience acceptance of the therapist's interpretation as equivalent to becoming the therapist, thereby losing his sense of himself as a separate person. As a result these sicker patients often defensively distance themselves from the therapist with resultant feelings of loneliness and disconnectedness.

THE BRITISH MIDDLE GROUP

In contrast with the Kleinians, certain members of the British Middle Group (Balint, Guntrip, Khan, and Winnicott) employ a largely noninterpretive technique during much of their work with very disturbed patients. Even this subgroup of the British Middle Group is rather heterogeneous and has not developed a mutually agreed-upon set of principles to accompany their object-relations theories of development. However, Winnicott (1954, 1963) has written in considerable detail about the management of regression in the course of the treatment of pre-Oedipal disturbances, and it is on his work that I will focus for the purposes of comparing analytic modes of handling projective identification. Winnicott feels that the cumulative trauma (Khan, 1963) resulting from repeated maternal impingements (Winnicott, 1952) makes it necessary for the infant or child to develop a defensively split sense of self consisting of a "true self" and a "false self" (Winnicott, 1960b). The false-self personality organization is that aspect of self that represents the sum of the defensive, self-protective, compliant adjustments that were developed in response to the mother's intrusion into the infant's spontaneous activity. Such intrusions or "impingements" interrupt the child's personal sense of "going on being" (Winnicott, 1963), that is, his sense of permanence and continuity of existence over time. The true self (those aspects of self that reflect the development of the child's unique qualities and individuality) becomes walled off and isolated from the functioning of the defensive false self. The latter aspects of self are often instrumental in achieving high levels of adaptation in academic and professional settings (Ogden, 1976), but these accomplishments are felt to be empty victories that leave the person feeling lonely, directionless, and unfulfilled (Fairbairn, 1940; Guntrip, 1969). Analysis of the earliest phases of development involve "a regression in search of the self" (Winnicott, 1954).

In the course of successful management of regression, the patient is able to relinquish reliance on false-self modes of defense (for example, endless compliance) by means of transferring onto the analyst the role of "caretaker" of, or "protective shield" for, the true self. In that setting of extreme emotional dependence, psychological development may proceed along lines different from the development of a defensive false-self personality organization. In this phase of work the analyst must provide the facilitating environment that was absent in the patient's childhood. Winnicott (1954) states that: "In the extreme case the therapist would need to go to the patient and actively present good mothering." Further, he notes:

> I have found that the patient has needed phases of regression to dependence in the transference, these giving experience of the full effect of adaptation to need that is in fact based on the analyst's

> (mother's) ability to identify with the patient (her baby). In the course of this kind of *experience* there is sufficient quantity of being merged in with the analyst to enable the patient to live and to relate without the need for [pathological] projective and introjective identificatory mechanisms. (Winnicott, reported by Khan, 1975, p. 27)

I would view the management of regression described above as based on a choice made by the analyst to participate fully in one of the patient's most fundamental unconscious fantasies that has become the basis of a powerful projective identification in the therapeutic relationship. The patient's unconscious fantasy of finding the longed-for good-enough mother in the analyst and the cared-for baby in himself is enacted interpersonally by means of a projective identification in which the internalized good-enough mother is in fantasy embodied by, and safely preserved in, the analyst, while the patient experiences himself as the loved and well-cared-for baby.

Balint (1968) correctly points out the way in which the regressed patient frequently becomes "addicted" to this good-enough mothering and sabotages the efforts of other aspects of himself to achieve a state of mature independence. Moreover, the patient will inevitably feel intensely angry and disappointed when the therapist stumbles in his efforts to provide good-enough mothering. Although this irrational aspect of the transference can be analyzed, the patient is not unjustified in his feeling that he has been tantalized by the illusion that good-enough mothering *for himself as an infant* can be found in the present adult therapeutic relationship. The analyst who has participated as recipient of this projective identification may develop corresponding feelings of anger at the patient for being unappreciative of the special lengths to which he is going in the therapy.

Despite these reservations about Winnicott's approach to the management of therapeutic regression, his contribution to the theory of the development of the early mother–infant dyad remains the essential framework for my own understanding of the clinical handling of projective identification. The rationale for much of the understanding of and response to the clinical phenomena presented in this volume is based on an outgrowth of Winnicott's ideas regarding the holding environment (1945, 1948, 1960a), impingement (1952), mirroring (1967, 1971), the capacity to be alone (1958), countertransference hatred (1947), and the objective countertransference (1947). From these ideas are derived the concepts of: (1) the centrality of countertransference analysis in the conduct of psychotherapy, and the use of the countertransference as a vehicle for understanding the transference; (2) the importance of the provision of a therapeutic setting in which the patient feels free to spontaneously explore his interpersonal environment, yet safe in the knowledge that there is an internal sanctuary (a private internality) to which he can retreat; and (3) psychological growth involving in the earliest stages, a two-person process in which the separate presence of one (the mother-therapist) is barely if at all recognized—much less appreciated—by the other (the infant-patient).

CLASSICAL ANALYSIS

Although not directly addressing the entire set of phenomena encompassed by the concept of projective identification, important classical contributions to our thinking about the interpersonal effects of one's unconscious psychological state include Anna Freud's (1936) concept of identification with the aggressor, Warren Brodey's (1965) notion of "externalization," Martin Wangh's (1962) "evocation of a proxy," and Sandler's (1976a, 1976b) "role actualization." On the whole, however, classical analysts have been slow to address the concept of projective identification, partially because it is difficult to conceptualize within the context of a theory that isolates the transference from the countertransference.

Classically, transference is defined in terms of the distortion of a present object representation on the basis of experience in a previous object relationship; one's feelings about a present object are altered in accordance with feelings originating in a previous relationship (Freud, 1912a, 1914a, 1915d). Thus, transference is conceptualized as an intrapsychic event that can be defined without reference to the way in which that event influences or is affected by the personality system of another person.

Similarly, countertransference is regularly viewed as an intrapsychic event generated by the analyst that is the counterpart of the transference, that is, the distortion of the analyst's view of and feelings about the patient based on the displacement and projection onto the patient of feelings arising in earlier relationships: "Countertransference is a transference reaction of an analyst to a patient" (Greenson, 1967, p. 348).

Freud, wary of the dangers inherent in the analyst's personal contribution to the psychoanalytic situation, and consequently to the psychoanalytic movement, took a cautious view of countertransference:

> We have become aware of the "countertransference," which arises in [the analyst] as a result of the patient's influence on his unconscious feelings, and we are almost inclined to insist that he shall recognize the countertransference in himself and overcome it. (1910, p. 144)

Annie Reich (1951, 1960, 1966), in what is one of the most fully developed contributions to the classical concept of countertransference, builds upon Freud's comments and conceptualizes countertransference as the interfering influence of "the analyst's own unconscious needs and conflicts on his understandings or technique" (1951, p. 26). Although she feels that countertransference feelings are inevitable, Reich sees these as sources of disruption of the analyst's capacity for empathy, trial identification, and evenly suspended attention.

The concept of countertransference in classical theory has become dynamically disconnected from that of transference, and there is little recognition of the component of countertransference that is complementary, to the transference, the part of the countertransference that is "the patient's creation" (Heimann, 1950). Without an understanding of this aspect of countertransference, there are no terms with which to conceptualize a process in which the therapist is pressured to *participate in* and *experience* aspects of the patient's internal object world. One regularly encounters in case presentations at scientific meetings and in the classical literature, the tacit assumption that a thorough analysis of the clinical material under discussion is possible without a single reference to what it feels like for the analyst to be with the patient or what the analyst has learned from the countertransference.[2]

Of course, there is much diversity of opinion with regard to countertransference within the classical analytic group. Although the views of Reich and Greenson are representative, there have been important contributions to the classical literature in which the countertransference (including the transferential level of the analyst's responses to the patient) is viewed as having a potentially constructive influence on the analytic process. (See, for example, Loewald, 1971, and particularly Boyer and Giovacchini, 1967, for their sensitive attentiveness to countertransference issues in their classical analytic treatment of schizophrenic patients.) Maxwell Gitelson's (1952) comments capture the thrust of a more encompassing classical view of countertransference, in which he acknowledges the potentially enriching influence of countertransference analysis on the two-person analytic process.

> The analyst must deal with [countertransferences] in himself, and together with his patient, he must deal with these when they

[2]In reading classical case reports, I have often been reminded of Winnicott's provocative statement: "There is no such thing as an infant" (1960a, p. 39). By this he meant that an infant cannot exist without a caretaking person, and therefore, the infant's experience and development are inextricably part of a two-person unit. Similarly, I have come to view transference as one facet of a two-person transference–countertransference system. Within that system, neither element can be meaningfully understood in isolation from the other.

> intrude into the analytic situation. . . . To the extent to which the analyst is himself open to their analysis and integration, he is in a real sense a vital participant in the analysis with the patient. It is this which constitutes the analyst's real contact with the patient and which lets the patient feel that he is not alone. (1952, p. 10)

Despite the awareness of Gitelson, Loewald, Boyer, Giovacchini, and others of the interactional context of the countertransference, there have been few efforts among classical analysts to generate a corresponding set of conceptualizations that might facilitate the analyst's thinking with regard to the specifics of the dynamic relationship between the transference and the countertransference. Recently, Weiss and Sampson (Weiss, 1971; Weiss et al., 1980) have proposed a "control mastery" theory (an outgrowth of classical ego psychology) that represents a significant contribution to this task.[3] The patient is seen by these analysts as unconsciously creating "test" situations in the interactions with the therapist that present the analyst with the same genetically determined psychological traumas that the patient is unconsciously attempting to master in the treatment. In this way the patient "turns passive into active," that is, the patient shifts from the position of the passive participant to that of the active one in a re-creation of the original traumatizing interaction.

In a "test" the patient creates an interpersonal situation in which he can unconsciously make an appraisal of the danger entailed in proceeding toward the realization of a specific unconscious wish or goal. Specifically, this appraisal involves the patient's unconscious assessment of whether he will be retraumatized by the therapist (as he was by his parents in his early development) if he were to diminish his reliance upon the defenses developed in response to the early trauma. Weiss and Sampson emphasize the growth-seeking (problem-solving)

[3]I am indebted to Dr. Marshall Bush for his comments on the discussion of control mastery theory presented in this chapter.

motivation for the patient's creation of a test situation (as opposed to a wish for drive discharge).

By means of a test, the patient unconsciously observes the analyst's ability to manage these genetically determined conflicts and selectively internalizes particular modes of mastery that are demonstrated in the analyst's method of handling the test situation. The patient in this way utilizes the test situation to "disconfirm pathogenic beliefs" that arose from his efforts to manage early trauma which are currently interfering with his pursuit of repressed developmental strivings (Bush, 1981). The introduction of this type of interactional point of view into classical technique represents an important advance in that it begins to create a perspective from which the countertransference can become data for understanding the transference. Implicit in this perspective is the idea that the qualities of many of the unconscious tests are understood by the analyst *in part* on the basis of the nature of the emotional strain that he finds himself experiencing with the patient. The patient often utilizes his unconscious capacities for accurate assessment of reality to design tests that take the analyst's psychological vulnerabilities as their focus, and this can create considerable emotional strain for the analyst.

A major difference between the control–mastery perspecitve and the theory of projective identification lies in the relative lack of emphasis in the former on the patient's unconscious projective fantasy of what he is "doing to" the analyst. Moreover, since these analysts have developed their ideas in the context of work with relatively healthy patients, unconscious blurring of self–object boundaries is not an essential feature of the form of interaction that they describe.

THE MODERN PSYCHOANALYTIC GROUP

Finally, I will briefly focus on a specialized technique termed "joining the resistance" that Nelson et al. (1968) and Spotnitz (1976) describe as an aspect of the analysis of narcissistic disorders. Although the members of the Modern Psychoanalytic Group do not conceptualize the clinical problems that they are addressing in terms of projective identification,[4] I feel that their work involves a noninterpretive mode of handling projective identification.

The technique of joining a resistance is based on "the therapist's utterance of statements which are consistent with the patient's irrational and defensive beliefs *whether or not these beliefs are openly stated as such*" (Sherman, 1968, p. 102, his italics). These analysts believe that the narcissistically fixated patient (including the borderline and schizophrenic patient) is unable to accept and integrate anything that is not felt to be an extension of himself. The analyst's interpretations are experienced as threatening and intrusive elements of non-self and therefore must be repelled. Rather than using verbal interpretation, these analysts assume various roles that correspond to the patient's unconscious defensive stances.

In this way, the patient is confronted in the therapy with externalized reflections of aspects of his own internal world. As the therapist becomes the embodiment of a defensive aspect of the patient, an interaction develops in which the patient has to contend with this aspect of himself in the person of the analyst. Spotnitz (1976) discusses the analyst's use of the countertransference in delineating for himself the nature of what is being projected into him.

In the course of interactions in which resistance has been joined, these authors contend, the patient is able to observe

---

[4]Among the principal contributors to the Modern Psychoanalytic Group are Selwyn Brody, Phyllis Meadow, Benjamin Nelson, Marie Coleman Nelson, Murray Sherman, Hyman Spotnitz, and Herbert Strean.

himself and accept his own understanding of (interpretation of) the aspect of himself represented by the therapist in a way that would not have been possible had the interpretation come from the analyst (non-self). This differs from psychodrama and role-playing therapies in that the role the therapist takes in joining a resistance is not determined by the problematic external life situation faced by the patient but by the nature of the patient's unconscious resistance.

A brief example from the work of Herbert Strean (1968) may serve to illustrate the resistance joining technique. Strean presents an excerpt from the treatment of a characterologically disturbed woman, frightened of being sexually exploited by men, all of whom she experienced as "animal-like" and overwhelming. This was understood as a projection of the patient's own intense, unconscious pre-Oedipal demands. The analyst was felt to be so selfish, demanding, and exploitative that the patient (Nancy) was on the verge of disrupting this, her fourth, therapy.

> [The analyst] told the patient . . . that he always liked to learn about his failures. Could she tell him what was wrong with him? "There must be something wrong with me to provoke you to leave!" Nancy responded triumphantly, "Yes, . . . you are a highly demanding spoiled brat, interested only in money and in sexual gratification . . . " Rather than interpret Nancy's projection her analyst said, "Maybe you're right. How do you think I got that way?"
>
> "You got that way because you were a disturbed child . . . You expect your patients to feed you all the time . . . "
>
> Nancy was complimented for her excellent diagnostic thinking and was asked what kind of a therapeutic plan should be devised for her therapist. "There you go again, always demanding something . . . You should be deprived and frustrated and given little . . . "
>
> Nancy continued her treatment. She gave the therapist strong doses of silence and then would interpret: "I know you are suffering, you are yearning to be fed, but this is good for you." When the therapist thought he would enact the role of a suffering, deprived child, Nancy would interrupt him and say, "That's

enough now! Curb your impulses. I'll let you talk when you deserve to do so."

Nancy was enacting the role of the frustrating parent who was putting the necessary controls on the demanding child. Because the therapist played the role of the child for Nancy, she was in reality treating the infantile part of her own character disorder. (pp. 184–185)

As is clear from this excerpt, role playing by the analyst is used to steer the therapeutic interaction. This differs from classical analysis which attempts to allow the transference to unfold at its own pace and in its own way with as little interference as possible. The modern analyst, on the basis of his assessment of the type of interaction that is needed by the patient, will "provoke a significant emotional interaction" of a specific type "to focus upon the consequent evolution of various roles and the meaning which grows from this process" (Sherman, 1968, p. 104).

I feel that this group of analysts, although using a different set of terms and not addressing the patient's unconscious fantasy of extrusion and control, are describing a way of returning to the patient a modified version of an unconscious defensive aspect of the patient that has been externalized by means of projective identification.

In evaluating role playing techniques designed to process projective identifications, one must keep in mind that the therapist pays a price for introducing manipulation into the therapeutic interaction in that the entire therapeutic interaction may lose its feeling of realness, genuineness, and honesty. It has been my experience that when enactment of the containment process is attempted (chapter 3), it is essential that the patient be clear that he is being invited by the therapist to engage in a type of play. When this is the case, as it usually seems to be in the work presented by the Modern Psychoanalytic Group, the framework of the therapy, the integrity of the therapist, and the dignity of the patient are all maintained.

5
THE DEVELOPMENTAL IMPACT OF EXCESSIVE MATERNAL PROJECTIVE IDENTIFICATION

The concept of identification has historically served as a vehicle for conceptualizing the interface between object relations and individual psychological organization. This has involved therapists and analysts in the task of coming to terms with their views about the ways in which the psychological attributes of one person are "taken in by" or "made a part of" another person (Fairbairn, 1952; Fraiberg et al., 1975; Freud, 1905, 1915b; Guntrip, 1961; Hartmann, 1939; Kernberg, 1966, 1976; Knight, 1940; Loewald, 1962; Schafer, 1968).

In this tradition the present chapter examines a form of identification demonstrated by a specific group of patients. This form of internalization will be explored to further refine the concept of identification and contribute to our thinking about the interplay of maternal pressures and the psychological processes of the infant.[1]

The clinical focus will be on one of this group of patients who demonstrate a form of identification with their mother and in particular with the conflicted aspects of the mother. These patients seem to take the mother's pathology, and especially the

[1]The terms *imitation, introjection,* and *identification* will be used to refer to types of internalization following the schema outlined by Schafer (1968).

mother's view of the patient as colored by her pathology, as a model for identification which is reflected in their self-representations, in their object relations, and in many of the characteristics of their ego organization. The early history of these patients is dominated by a picture of a mother deeply involved in her own problems—problems from which she failed to shield the infant.[2] Among the group of patients studied, examples of such maternal preoccupations include: one mother who was consumed by wishes for the child to be an embodiment of an aspect of herself which was both intensely hated and highly idealized; another mother who was filled with the need for the baby to restore her relationship with her mother, who had died when she was 10 years old; and finally, a mother consumed by wishes and fears concerning the sex of the child because of her own wishes, fears, and disappointments about her own sex.

Such circumstances become pathogenic when the mother's attempts to deal with her problems interfere with her ability to respond empathically to her child. Such interference may occur under conditions where the mother, in her attempts to deal with consciously unacceptable feelings, develops excessive reliance on such psychological processes and modes of behavior as splitting, denial, projective identification, and impulsive activity.

A clinical discussion of the process of internalization of the conflicted psychological state of the mother will be used as a vehicle to formulate a developmental hypothesis regarding this identification, and to offer some thoughts about this specific use of early identification as a defensive response to excessive maternal projective identification.

---

[2]In this volume "early history" is not viewed as a static fact that is slowly discovered but rather as a dynamic construction, which patient and therapist work toward and which is based on the patient's changing retrospective view as well as on the unfolding data of the transference and countertransference.

CASE HISTORY

Miss R., a 34-year-old single woman born in Wales, was working as a secretary in a large American city when she decided to seek psychotherapy. Life had become "unbearable" as a result of her desperate longing for a boyfriend who had just broken off their relationship. Unable to live without him, she felt on the verge of suicide. The patient thought constantly about this man who had let her down. Miss R. ruminated about the things she might have done to prevent the breakup and the ways she could possibly get him to take her back.

This was the fourth time in 12 years that the patient had been involved in a very intense, dependent relationship that had ended this way. She had been treated for a year in psychotherapy after the third of these relationships. That therapy was terminated when the therapist left the area. Eighteen months later, the patient sought therapy for a second time.

Miss R. appeared considerably older than 34 and gave the appearance of being a rather old-fashioned, slightly untidy woman who had somehow refused to accept the fact that times had changed. She looked drained and tired; her eyes were red, presumably from crying and lack of sleep.

Since Miss R. was 18 years old she had been filled with the conscious wish to find a man who loved her and could alleviate her intense feelings of longing and incompleteness. The involvements that dominated the patient's adult life were all so similar that a description of one can serve for all four.

Soon after the end of the previous therapy, the patient became involved with a lawyer who had had a long series of short, unsuccessful relationships with women. The patient knew this about the man but blinded herself to the fact that he did not express any affection for her. Miss R. became more and more clinging and demanding of his affection, until he told her after 14 months that she was "too much for him" and ended the relationship. The patient appeared at his office begging him to take her back and telephoned him several times a day. She cried at work, took frequent sick days, and finally was dismissed.

On the basis of talks with her mother (the circumstances of which are described below), as well as through discussions with her father and maternal grandfather, the patient gradually constructed the following history, which she presented over the course of the beginning stages of therapy. Miss R. was the eldest of three children born to a lower-middle-class family in urban Wales. The patient's mother, Mrs. R., was a strikingly attractive woman who had had a series of successes in amateur singing competitions in London before she married. She was considered very talented and had fantasies of becoming a famous opera singer. However, at 23 she felt old and thought that she had already lost her chance for a successful operatic career.

Mrs. R. had been raised by two alcoholic parents who could barely provide the essentials of life for their two children. From the age of 9, Mrs. R. worked to buy relatively expensive clothes for herself and her brother in order to create the impression that she came from a middle-class family. She daydreamed of having immense wealth and of marrying a diplomat or a man of royal lineage.

While in London the patient's mother met and, after 6 months, married a man who had recently inherited a family business in Wales. Upon returning to Wales, they discovered that the business had faltered and was nearly bankrupt. Two months after the marriage, the patient was conceived. The infant was seen as a quiet, "easy" baby. Breast-feeding was continued for 16 months. In these early months the patient's mother seemed to enjoy the closeness of the breast-feeding situation, during which she would sing to the infant.

The patient believed that this relationship changed drastically once she was weaned. From then on the mother was described as having been a very powerful, angry woman who could be ruthless in her attacks on the patient. The patient had vivid memories, dating back to a time before she was 4, of being treated with disdain and disgust and of having been told over and over that she was incorrigibly stupid, unlikable, and exceedingly ugly. In the mother's mind the distastefulness of these traits was compounded by their apparent close resemblance to the traits of the patient's father. The mother treated her husband with contempt and ceaselessly criticized him for his ineptitude and lack of manliness. The father remained very much to himself, hardly involving himself with his children.

The patient developed a quiet somberness and was often stubborn, but never defiant. Miss R. remembered her childhood as a continual barrage of verbal attacks from a mother whose venom seemed to increase instead of subside with each assault.

Mrs. R. would periodically withdraw into severe depression, sometimes lasting for months at a time. During these periods, she would cease to care for her own appearance (which she highly prized at other times) and would neglect the cleaning of the house and the preparation of meals. Instead, she spent most of her time in bed talking to herself and to the patient about how worthless, old, and unattractive she felt.

From early school age, Miss R. was interested in music and dance and was recognized at school as having talent. When the patient performed in school programs, Mrs. R. consistently refused to attend. The patient's fantasies of becoming a famous ballerina elicited rage from the mother who would accuse her of living in a dream world.

The patient's mother repeatedly threatened to send her to live with an aunt in London. At the age of 6, and again at the age of 9, Miss R. was sent to London for a period of a month when the mother could "bear it no longer." Then, when the patient was 11, without warning, the mother moved away with a man 10 years her junior. She returned after 6 months, disappointed and defeated. Shortly thereafter, the patient and her family emigrated to America. The verbal attacks on Miss R. continued until the patient left home at age 18. Having done well in secondary school, the patient was accepted at a university. However, her parents refused to pay the tuition, even though they could have afforded it, and in the end the patient moved to another city, where she began working as a secretary. A few years later, she became involved in the first of the four relationships that dominated the succeeding years of her life.

Miss R. insisted that she had found her previous therapy extremely helpful and would "do anything" to be treated again. In the twice-weekly therapy to be presented here, the patient very soon established a pattern of filling the hours with detailed descriptions of the latest insults, embarrassments, and humiliations that she had suffered at the hands of her most recent boyfriend. These monologues were intertwined with repetitive accounts of her intense longing for this same man and the feeling that she could not go on without him. The descriptions were delivered in a monotonous, persistent tone that did not reflect any ability to distance herself from the material or understand it. In addition, the patient managed to communicate the fierce tenacity with which she would hold onto this mode of relating.

As the therapist began to feel he understood some aspect of the transference or some other part of the patient's communication, he would venture a clarification or occasionally an interpretation. Such interventions were consistently met with indifference, and the patient would go on with her descriptions in precisely the same way as she had before the intervention. For example, in the third month of treatment, the patient spent large portions of a number of sessions mechanically and repetitively describing a bout of shingles that she had had a year before beginning therapy. In the course of this narrative, Miss R. talked about how callously several doctors had treated her. She said that she had had this kind of experience with doctors all through her life. "I've always hated their patronizing, their use of their knowledge and position to belittle others and to boost their own egos. I could never relax with any of them and always felt humiliated by them." As this theme was repeated in several sessions, the patient at one point made a slip and substituted the therapist's name for that of one of the earlier doctors. Later in the session the therapist said, "I wonder if you sometimes feel that I can be a patronizing, belittling, humiliating doctor?" The patient, without pause or hesitation, responded that the therapist was a psychiatrist and that she was referring to internists. In the same breath, the patient began a lengthy description of an incident in her adolescence when a dermatologist had paraded her in front of a group of medical students so they could examine her severe case of facial acne.

Gradually, after several more weeks of this form of interaction, the therapist began to stop the patient when she attempted to ignore what had been said and would ask her to consider the way that she had of not giving any evidence of having "held" or "taken in" what had been said even for a moment. This intervention in turn would be ignored or paid momentary lip service, and the patient would return to another monologue as if nothing had been said. In the same way, the patient responded with bewilderment when her repeated lateness to her sessions was treated as worthy of exploration for possible meaning.

This form of interaction continued for 6 months, during which the therapist struggled to understand the meaning underlying this transference-countertransference pattern. The therapist would often feel tormented by the patient's relentless, monotonous, lifeless descriptions, frequently feeling trapped in seemingly endless therapy hours. Sometimes, he felt as if he were utterly helpless in the hands of a robot, without any hope of appealing to a responsive human core. At other times, he imagined himself taking the patient by the throat and sadistically jolting her from her lifeless discourses. It was when these sadistic fantasies were at their peak that the therapist felt the greatest impulse to flee from the room. At the same time as the therapist was becoming aware of these countertransference feelings, he also noted a recurrent theme in the patient's monologues. The patient began to talk almost exclusively about her mother's threats to abandon her and the three different occasions when she actually did so.

The awareness of the transference-countertransference themes described and their link to the theme of abandonment led the therapist to say to the patient: "I get the feeling that the repetitive descriptions you bring to each session are in ways an attack on me, an effort to goad me into attacking you in precisely the way your mother used to do. Maybe there would be some comfort in that for you. After all, at least you knew your mother was there when she was attacking you."

A subtle shift occurred at this point. The patient seemed not to be moved by this interpretation, any more than she had been by earlier interventions, but for the first time something different happened in the therapy. In the succeeding sessions, Miss R. continued with her monotonous descriptions with one important change: she no longer looked at the therapist. The patient's impact on the therapist was no longer simply one of torment; there was a glimpse of some other element in it. In retrospect, it seemed that this element had been present in the earlier phase of work but had been more thoroughly masked by the intensity of feeling involved in the tormentor–tormented aspect of the interaction. Even though the form of the repetitive descriptions remained the same, there were subtle, almost subliminal shifts in the nature of the interpersonal interaction. The patient no longer nodded at the therapist as she walked to her chair at the beginning of the session; she made no reference to the content of previous meetings; her dreams were very vague and contained only one person, herself. The therapist found himself struggling to maintain the sense of himself as the tormented object in preference to the increasingly chilling and disorienting feeling that was being fostered in him—the feeling of his not being there at all.

Even though this awareness of the struggle was helping the therapist to clarify for himself the nature of the therapeutic interaction, the therapist did not immediately offer this to the patient in the form of an interpretation. It was felt that the resistance to such an idea was still very powerful, and that the therapeutic alliance was fragmentary.

The therapist was able, however, to make use of this understanding in his handling of the material that the patient was offering. Over the next several months, as Miss R. talked about the tormented feelings she had had in her relationships with her boyfriends and her mother, the therapist was attuned both to the way the mother was felt to be more securely present in a tormented–tormenting relationship and to the way the patient herself felt more recognized, more present, more real for her mother at those times.

Very slowly the patient's descriptions of the mother's torment began to reflect a distance on the material. Miss R. for the first time was able to tell the therapist about the infrequent but highly significant periods of calm in the storm of maternal torment: it had been very important to Mrs. R. that the patient and no one else look at her photograph album with her. At these times, the patient's mother took on a softness and youthfulness that she displayed at no other occasion. They would spend hours admiring photographs and newspaper clippings from the era of the mother's amateur singing competitions and the patient's early infancy. Mrs. R. would sing in a way that the patient genuinely admired and felt soothed by. She said she felt "aglow" at these special times. In fact, she took on a gentleness in the therapy hours as she quietly talked about the way she had felt special to her mother at those times, as if there were something about herself that the mother could not do without. But these times with her mother had had abrupt endings leaving the patient feeling as if she (Miss R.) had disappeared afterward.

It was at this point in the therapy, just when a therapeutic alliance seemed to be developing, that the patient became increasingly anxious, developed migraine headaches and nausea, and began to cancel sessions. It took a long time before Miss R. was able to say that she had become very frightened of talking openly to the therapist because she had "known" from the beginning that there was a secretary in another division of the clinic whom she knew socially, who had access to her records and had been reading them. She knew this because the secretary had made reference to Miss R. being over 30, and there was no other way she could have known that other than from the records. Since in the therapist's view the patient appeared to be well over 30, this suggested that Miss R.'s suspicions may not have been founded in reality. The therapist explored with the patient the basis of her belief that the secretary had seen her records. In the following session, the therapist said that he had found on looking into the record-keeping practices of the clinic that it was highly unlikely that the secretary could have had access to the patient's records, but that it would be naive to say that any records are totally immune to vandalism. The patient sullenly said that she had half-expected to be publicly humiliated when she came to any clinic, and that she guessed she would just have to live with that danger.

Over the next few weeks of therapy, the patient was able to address the transference level of her anxieties. She noted that although she had had fears about doctors and breaches of confidentiality prior to the beginning of the therapy, not until she began talking about and reexperiencing in the therapy the moments of feeling aglow did she begin to be overwhelmed by her fears of exposure. She said that she felt that the core of her worries was a fear of being found out, of being exposed as different from what she appeared to be. She talked about fantasies and dreams that she had had since childhood of being exposed as utterly and basically fraudulent. It was not so much that there was a horrible crime that she was keeping hidden; rather, it was the act of deception itself that was the crime.

As this was being discussed, Miss R.'s anxiety and somatization subsided. The patient went on to relate the feeling of being exposed to earlier feelings that she had had with her mother. She could understand the feeling being present at the "special" times with her mother because to be that special was such a fragile and tenuous situation in the midst of all that had happened before and all that was sure to happen afterward. How long could it be before the mother would see the patient for what she was? What was surprising to the patient was the awareness of the same fear of exposure during the mother's torment. The patient began to be aware that there too she felt the danger of exposure. For how long could she really be the living embodiment of worthlessness and ugliness for the mother to rave at?

At this point the therapist could make use of his experience in the countertransference to say: "You must have struggled desperately to be a child your mother could despise and torment, because you must have been afraid that if you weren't, you would have ceased to exist for her at all."

Over the next year of the therapy—which lasted two years in all—the patient's fear of becoming nonexistent appeared and reappeared in the transference, in the patient's outside relationships, and in the patient's increasing understanding of her early relationship with her mother. During a series of sessions in the middle of the second year of the therapy the patient reexperienced an eerie feeling that she had not thought much about since she was a child, although the feeling had not been an uncommon one for her. It was only through her description of a group of memory images that she could convey to the therapist any sense of the feeling that she was experiencing.

In each of these memories, the patient pictured herself in a dimly lit room watching her mother doing something, while her mother was unaware that the patient was in the room. The mother was pictured as being lost in her thoughts as she sat listening to the radio, or cleaning the silverware, or smoking a cigarette. The patient became extremely anxious in the therapy hours as she remembered these scenes. Miss R. said that she hated the eerie feeling associated with these memories, and that she could hear a thin, high-pitched, "empty" sound that went along with the feeling. The patient said that the sound ought to be used in a science fiction movie about outer space. The sound somehow reminded her of a large, clean, empty stainless steel container that did not "even have any fingerprints on it." The feelings of outer-space-like aloneness and sterile emptiness that Miss R. had often felt when she was with her mother were powerfully felt in the therapy hours over a period of several months. At times the patient said she felt nauseated by these feelings and was afraid that she would leave the hour and only be able to remember the therapist as a man in a semidarkened room, lost in thought and unaware that she had been sitting with him during the sessions.

Many of the issues dominating this phase of the work were brought into clearer focus in a session that followed the patient's viewing *The Wizard of Oz* on television. In that hour Miss R. described how terrified she had been of the movie when she was a child. She said that during the previous evening while watching the film she had been very moved at the end when Dorothy finds that the Wizard is a little, bald-headed man and in a rage of disappointment shouts at him, "You're a very wicked man." The Wizard says, "No, Dorothy, I'm not a very good wizard, but I'm not a bad man." The patient sobbed bitterly and said, "I'm like the Wizard. I wasn't as special as she needed me to be or as ugly as she needed me to be. If I wasn't a wizard, I was nothing to her."

In the months of therapy that followed, various aspects of this early relationship were expressed in the transference. At one point, the patient began to feel she had some very special importance for the therapist, perhaps as a star patient. In the midst of this the patient became very anxious and in one session asked the therapist to authorize in writing that her lateness to work on a given morning had been due to her therapy session. Upon analyzing this request the patient became aware that her reason for the request was the feeling that she was so unreal to the therapist that he would not be able to remember her name without consulting his records. At other times, there was intense despondency between sessions, stemming from the feeling that she did not exist for the therapist when she was not with him.

This material was discussed in terms of the patient's feeling that she did not exist for her mother other than as the ugly, stubborn, villainous child the mother needed to torment and despise, or the child who could reflect the glow of the mother's feelings about herself in the photograph album.

As the profound sadness of these ideas was discussed, the patient grew increasingly free with her anger, an emotion that had been almost totally absent before. Formerly, anger had to be disavowed, as in her attribution of her lateness to events outside her control. The patient had also tended to somatize (migraine headaches and nausea) or feel suicidal at times when one would have expected her to have felt angry. Very gradually, the patient became more and more able to express her resentment toward her mother for having used her "to be her wicked and wonderful wizard." Miss R. could also say that she did not intend to be a special patient for the therapist any more, and that he would have to find someone else to do that for him. This change could be discussed as a reflection of the fact that the patient was no longer afraid to acknowledge the separateness of herself and her mother-therapist. Formerly, feelings different from those appropriate to the "wizard" had been experienced as threatening to expose her as being other than simply a reflection of her mother's or of her therapist's needs and fantasies.

There was also the feeling of freshly discovering people and things around her. She complimented and criticized the therapist for the selection of pictures in his office and noticed new clothes that he wore. She also seemed to discover herself as a physical being and began to dress and wear her hair much more age-appropriately and stylishly. Again, this was understood in terms of the patient's ability to acknowledge and even enjoy a sense of her own separateness without feeling in danger of becoming nonexistent for the internalized mother or for the therapist as a result of being separate from each.

PROJECTIVE IDENTIFICATION AND IMPINGEMENT

Projective identification constituted an important dimension of the therapeutic interaction between Miss R. and her therapist, and the latter's awareness of this was central to his understanding of his countertransference responses to the patient. For example, Miss R. relied heavily on projective identification in her efforts to master the internalized tormenting-tormented relationship with her mother. For a long period of time, the patient projected the internalized, tormented child into the therapist, while she herself adopted a strong identification with her tormenting mother. In so doing, Miss R. felt she had rid herself of an unwanted part of herself and succeeded in turning the therapist into the tormented child.

This was not simply a fantasy, since the patient's mode of relating elicited a very strong countertransference response in the therapist, in which he felt powerless to be anything other than the object of torment for the patient. The therapist fantasied that the only alternative to being the tormented object was to become nonexistent for the patient. At other times the therapist felt that fleeing from the room (thus ending the relationship) would be the only way to oppose the immense pressure to be the tormented object for the patient.

Later the therapist came to understand the patient's projective identification as a defense against reexperiencing in the transference the painful awareness of separateness from the mother-therapist. Only through his awareness of his feelings as responses to the patient's projective identifications was the therapist able to make use of this material to understand the patient and avoid acting on or closing off his feelings. In part, it was the therapist's analysis of these countertransference responses that allowed the patient to reinternalize the projected aspect of herself in a modified form—a form she could accept as a part of herself and analyze and integrate in the second year of therapy.

The history, recovered memories, and transference-countertransference patterns offered important data regarding the unique qualities of the failure of maternal responsiveness that were internalized by the patient.[3] The history is replete with examples of the mother's difficulty in responding to those aspects

[3]It must be borne in mind that the "failures of maternal responsiveness" that we learn about through our work with our patients are necessarily reflections of the subjective experience of the patient and do not necessarily bear a one-to-one correspondence to an objective assessment of the mother's capacity for empathy. Despite the fact that we are always viewing the patient's past through the lens of the patient's subjectivity, reconstruction remains an important part of analytic work.

of the patient's needs, wishes, and interests that were not simply extensions of what the mother needed the patient to be.

The patient poignantly portrayed in the transference aspects of her early experience with maternal impingement. The patient had been noticeably relaxed in the sessions for several weeks in the beginning of the second year of therapy and seemed to be getting considerable pleasure and satisfaction from the meetings. In the session that marked the end of this period, the patient came in, sat down, and immediately began to cry. The therapist asked her what was wrong. She explained that she had just been yelled at by her boss at work. She then told the therapist to go on with what he had in mind for that day's session, adding that she did not want to interfere with what he had planned for that meeting.

The therapist was stunned by this and said, "You're saying that you feel I have a plan for each session that I need to get through at any cost, and that my plans have nothing at all to do with anything you happen to be feeling?" The patient said that was right and was curious why the therapist had called it a feeling of hers, when she felt that it was a fact.

This theme recurred over and over again in different forms. Since the therapist was reasonably certain that he was not being unresponsive to the patient, the material could be understood as a set of feelings portraying early experiences of maternal impingement. The patient was gradually able to view such interactions with the therapist as a re-creation of her own relationship with her mother, wherein gratification of specific maternal needs was substituted for an empathic responsiveness to the child's internal state.

The history that Miss R. presents and the therapeutic relationship she established offer ample evidence of the presence of an intense, circumscribed mother-daughter interdependence. This interdependence can be understood as having been based on the projection of maternal pathology in such a way that highly circumscribed aspects of the relationship with the child took on critical importance, leaving the mother virtually oblivious to and unresponsive to qualities and aspects of the child that lay outside the "beam" of the projected maternal pathology (Greenacre, 1959). As described above, Miss R.'s mother oscillated between intense feelings of glowing grandiosity and equally intense feelings of worthlessness and self-hatred. Both of these sets of feelings became the basis for a powerful projective identification, with the patient as recipient. While the patient was acting in congruence with these projective identifications, aspects of the patient were terribly important to her mother, but the scope of these projective identifications was limited. The patient felt that, at those times when she was unable to be the embodiment of the projected aspect of the mother, she ceased to exist for her mother.

To summarize, Miss R. presented a picture of her mother as a powerful woman who needed her child to be a reflection of a specific aspect of her own pathology—the wicked or the wonderful wizard. More specifically, the mother's pathology seemed to be characterized by a splitting of self- and object-representations into idealized and denigrated parts. This splitting was maintained by means of projective identification and was reflected in her to-and-fro movement from idealization of self and object to feelings of worthlessness and despair. The analysis of the transference and the countertransference suggested that the patient had felt real for the mother only when she was in a tormented-tormenting relationship, and that she had clung to this form of relatedness in preference to the sense of not existing for the mother. A basic anxiety for the patient with her mother, with her boyfriends, and in the therapy was a fear of being exposed as different from what she was in the mother's projective fantasies. If this were to happen, Miss R. feared, she would be outside the realm of what was meaningful to the mother and that outside this "beam" she would be unmothered and dangerously unprotected. Any acknowledgment of separateness from the mother's fantasy of the patient was experienced as a threat to the relative safety of the equilibrium wherein the patient was for her mother what her mother needed her to be.

THE DEVELOPMENT OF A DEFENSIVE IDENTIFICATION

In viewing internalization of maternal pathology from a developmental perspective, the discussion must immediately center around the changing pattern of the ways in which the mother and child perceive one another. At the beginning, the good-enough mother and her infant feel to one another as if they are a single unit (Mahler, 1968; Spitz, 1965; Winnicott, 1956). There is no inside or outside, self or other. The mother's role is to be responsive to the infant's emotional and physiological needs and in so doing create the illusion that the infant and mother are one. The wished-for breast is there when it is wanted and in precisely the way that it is wanted because that is the nature of things.

Miss R. gives us some indication that her mother was a good-enough mother at this early stage and could take genuine pleasure in caring for her infant and in responsively meeting the infant's needs. In addition, there is evidence for an early period of good-enough mothering in the therapeutic relationship. Miss R. was extremely adept at creating a holding environment for the therapist for a brief time while he was ill: in a tender and humorous way, the patient expressed her concern for the therapist in a card in which she parodied Welsh home medical remedies.

On the road to developing the capacity to differentiate self and object, the mother helps the infant create transitional objects and phenomena (Winnicott, 1951). The transitional object is at once an object created and magically controlled by the infant and an object separate from him. The question of which it is, is never asked because it is both, in such a way as to make the question never arise. As soon as there is an awareness of the question, the child is on his way to recognizing the object as separate. Mrs. R.'s ability to help the patient create a transitional realm of experience was hampered by the intrusion of her own pathology into her efforts at empathy. The patient gives us evidence that her mother ceased to be a responsively flexible medium (a mirror) and instead reflected the very definite features of her own conflicted and poorly integrated internal state. The subjective object was prematurely given definite shape that denied the infant the illusion that she herself had created it. This resulted in a premature awareness of the separateness of the infant and mother which the infant could not tolerate.

Miss R.'s internalization of maternal pathology may be understood in terms of a specific mode of defense employed by the infant in her attempt to protect herself against the premature recognition of separateness imposed on her by excessive maternal projective identification. The infant struggled to maintain the illusion that it was *she herself,* and not an outside object with motives and wishes different from her own, that she was sensing in the maternal impingements. The child attempted to create the illusion that her spontaneous gesture was characterized specifically by those qualities of the mother's pathology that were communicated through the nature of the projective identifications. She struggled to maintain the crumbling illusion that it was she who created the conflicted moods and feelings that she was perceiving, even though this was at variance with the sense that she was coming upon something that had nothing to do with her.

This defensive illusion is not at all equivalent to the creation of the normal transitional object, which is characterized by the irrelevance of the question, "Is it me or not-me?" In her desperate attempts to deny her perception of separateness, she took the mother's pathology (communicated by means of projective identification) as the basic mark of herself and modeled her self- and object-representations according to it. The anxiety underlying the fiercely stubborn allegiance to the character structures that evolved in this way is the terror of reexperiencing the feeling of being prematurely separate from the mother and subject to feelings of intense helpessness and a sense of being dangerously exposed and unprotected.

On the basis of this developmental formulation, I feel that

we can conceptualize the internalization under study as a distinctive form of identification. As with other forms of identification, it involves a process in which the infant modifies his self-representations and patterns of behavior in an effort to make himself like the perceived object (Schafer, 1968). This particular form of identification is distinguished by the following characteristics: (1) the identification originates as a specific defensive response to maternal projective identification in an effort to deny the separateness of self and object; (2) the qualities of the projective identification that are internalized are taken as the basic mark of the self and used as a model for the development of object relations, self-representations, and other internal structures.

From this perspective the observations of Ritvo and Solnit (1958), based on a Yale Child Study Center longitudinal study, become particularly relevant. They reported that identifications seem to develop in the service of defense rather than in the service of adaptation when an infant's inborn characteristics collide "forcefully with the deepiest conflicts in the mother" (p. 81). "The child imitated the mother *in toto* and in this way perfected a controllable, kinesthetic image of the mother to replace the threatening representation of the mother" (p. 82). What was imitated was not simply the mother, but the mother in a state of distress in which her pathology was most graphically expressed. It is significant that their findings relate the observation of conflict-laden maternal handling of the infant to the appearance in the child of a form of identification that was felt to function in the service of defense and that took the form of a total imitation of the mother in a state of conflict.

The particular defensive identification under discussion can be understood as arising out of a failure of the mother to adequately shield the infant from her pathology, thereby exposing the infant to a premature awareness of the object as separate. The infusion of the internalized representation of the maternal conflict into so many aspects of the developing psychological structures and organizations of the infant reflects both the massive effort to deny the separateness and the very malleable and incomplete nature of the infant's psyche at the stage in question. The aim is not to model the self after an external object in order to emulate it; rather, it is an effort to modify the internal structures in order to deny the perception that the object is different from the self. For this reason the aspects of self and ego modeled in this way are not sources of pride, strength, or well-being; instead, they are felt to be fragile and sensitive areas that can tolerate no inspection lest the disguise cease to function, leaving the patient exposed to the knowledge of the separateness of the mother.

SUMMARY

A defensive form of internalization stemming from the impact on the infant of excessive maternal projective identification has been discussed. This internalization took the form of an identification with the conflicted aspect of the mother and influenced the development of the patient's self-representations, qualities of ego and superego functioning, and object relations. A developmental hypothesis was proposed in which the infant was seen as having experienced premature awareness of the mother as a separate person as a result of the mother's excessive reliance on projective identification as a mode of relatedness and form of psychological defense. In the child's attempt to defend herself against such disturbing awareness of separateness, she struggled to maintain the illusion that it was herself and not the mother that she was perceiving in the projected maternal pathology. The result was a strong defensive identification with the projected aspects of the mother. The motivation for this identification was powerfully enhanced by the fact that the child felt real for the mother only when in the "beam" of her pathology, that is, only when behaving in a way that was congruent with the mother's projective identifications. The development of this type of defensive identification is understood as representing one of a variety of possible pathological adaptations to excessive maternal projective identification.

6
PSYCHIATRIC HOSPITAL TREATMENT

THE INPATIENT SETTING

The clinical usefulness of the concept of projective identification has been studied primarily in the context of outpatient individual psychotherapy. In this chapter we will examine projective identifications as it occurs in inpatient treatment. Inpatient psychiatric work entails a broadened and less well defined framework of treatment and is powerfully influenced by the social system of the psychiatric hospital within which the treatment takes place.

In this chapter, several complementary lines of thought concerning analytic inpatient work are discussed. Case material will be presented which demonstrates the value of the concept of projective identification as a framework for organizing and dynamically formulating the complex interplay between the intrapsychic and the interpersonal sphere. Finally, there will be a discussion of two additional facets of projective identification as they relate to hospital treatment: projective identification occurring in a group setting and the accessibility to action in inpatient treatment.

Even when the most strenuous efforts are made in a psychiatric hospital to isolate individual psychotherapy from the rest of the patient's treatment, such efforts are never wholly successful and usually result in self-defeating efforts on the part of all concerned to maintain an illusion of "analytic purity." Much more commonly the individual psychotherapy is seen as one facet of a patient's hospital treatment that must in some way be integrated with the overall therapy program. Often the therapist is either a member of the inpatient staff, or a consultant. As a staff member, the therapist will participate in a variety of ward meetings, some of which will also be attended by the patient. In addition, the therapist and the patient not uncommonly happen upon one another on the ward or the hospital grounds and sometimes exchange glances, nods, and conversation. Much more frequently than in outpatient work, the therapist will receive phone calls from, and will consult with, members of the patient's family.

The therapist will frequently also have significant influence over such basic matters as what the patient is allowed to eat, what medications are given, when and with whom the patient is allowed to leave the hospital grounds, when the patient will be discharged, and so forth. In addition, the therapist will have relationships with other staff members, which will inevitably involve rivalries, power struggles, sexual attractions, and friendships. The patient will frequently have some direct or indirect knowledge of these relationships. Further, both patient and therapist exist within the social organization of the hospital and are subject to the strains and integrative trends within and between parts of the organization. It is this complex and somewhat loosely defined framework of inpatient treatment that is the context of the present study.

CONCEPTUAL FRAMEWORK

Several overlapping and complementary lines of thought have developed over the past 50 years that deal with the application of psychoanalytic principles to an understanding of interactions occurring in the context of a psychiatric hospital. The earliest of these papers discusses the propensity of the patient in a hospital setting to externalize unconscious conflicts by splitting transferences toward the therapist and displacing one or the other aspect of these feelings onto various members of the hospital staff (Bullard, 1940; Knight, 1936; Menninger; 1936; Reider, 1936; Simmel, 1929).

This phenomenon is seen both as an opportunity to view and to understand the patient's unconscious conflicts and resistances to treatment and as a threat to the staff's ability to maintain therapeutic distance. The emphasis in the line of thought contained in these early papers is almost entirely on the projection of the patient's unconscious wishes and conflicts, with very little acknowledgment of the staff members' conscious or unconscious contributions to the interpersonal field.

A second line of thought, initiated by Harry Stack Sullivan (1930–31, 1956), focuses on a conception of the hospital as a place where staff members collectively strive to create interpersonal conditions in which the patient might dare to expand ("by experience") his underdeveloped capacities for meaningful connectedness with other human beings. There is an emphasis on the staff's unconscious intrapsychic and interpersonal limitations which contribute to the hospital's failure to offer the patient adequate treatment (see also Fromm-Reichmann, 1937, 1950). Otto Will (1970, 1975) and Harold Searles (1963, 1975), in discussing their long-term work with hospitalized schizophrenic patients, emphasize the importance of the therapist's capacity to perceive and acknowledge the range of feelings he experiences with a patient and to integrate his understanding of the patient's contribution to these feelings into his responses to the patient.

A third line of thought has developed that integrates an interactional frame of reference with a social-systems approach (Parsons, 1937, 1951, 1957). Interpersonal relations within a hospital are seen as involving a dynamic interplay between conscious and unconscious feeling states on the part of both staff members and patients (Adler, 1973; Caudill, 1958; Freeman,

1953). In addition, the qualities of the hospital organization, structure, leadership, intergroup pressures, relation of the hospital to the community, etc., are viewed as the context for and major contributing influence to any interpersonal field existing within the hospital (Edelson, 1970; Greenblatt et al., 1957; Jones, 1953; Stanton & Schwartz, 1954; Stotland & Kobler, 1965).

The three lines of thought emerging from the literature can be united into a framework for approaching interactions occurring within a psychiatric hospital. That framework would include: (1) the patient's conscious and unconscious system of motivations and meanings; (2) the conscious and unconscious system of motivations and meanings of the staff that are activated in the course of interactions with the patients and with other staff members, both individually and in groups; (3) the conflicts and integrative trends within and between the subsystems of a hospital organization and the relationship between the subsystems and the overall hospital organization; and (4) the capacity of staff members and patients for self-observation, for self-understanding (including an understanding of one's place in a social system), and for psychological and interpersonal growth.

Projective identification is a concept uniquely suited to address each of the facets of this framework in a unifying way. Separately, the concepts of projection and identification focus almost entirely on shifts within the intrapsychic sphere, that is, shifts in the thoughts, feelings, and fantasies of one person. Projection refers specifically to the *intrapsychic process* of disowning aspects of one's self-representations. Similarly, the concept of identification addresses the way in which one modifies one's self-representations and patterns of motivation and behavior in accordance with features of an object-representation (Schafer, 1968). There is nothing intrinsic to the concept that deals with the role played in this process by the personality system of the recipient.

Therapists and analysts from a wide range of analytic schools have attempted to generate ways of thinking that would encompass both the intrapsychic and interpersonal components of the framework for approaching interactions in a hospital setting. Brodey's concept of "externalization" (1965), Wangh's "evocation of a proxy" (1962), Winnicott's "impingement" (1952) and "mirroring" (1967), Greenacre's "focal symbiosis" (1959), Bion's "container and the contained" (1967), and Sandler's "role actualization" (1976a, 1976b), represent only a very partial listing of psychoanalytic formulations of the interplay between the intrapsychic and the interpersonal. Each of these conceptualizations can be understood as a particularly clear statement of an aspect of the larger concept of projective identification. The latter concept provides a way of organizing our thinking about the relationship between conscious and unconscious fantasy, interpersonal evocation ("externalization" or "actualization"), containment by the object, and reinternalization (via identification or introjection).

Clinical material will now be presented to demonstrate the operational use of the concept of projective identification as a tool for understanding specific types of complex and often bewildering interactions that occur in a hospital setting. The interactions described occurred on two different, analytically oriented inpatient services.

CLINICAL VIGNETTE I

Mr. F. was a 25-year-old man diagnosed as schizophrenic who had been hospitalized for about one and a half years on a long-term analytically oriented ward when he began treatment with a female psychiatric resident, Dr. W. Dr. W. would be seeing this patient in intensive, individual therapy for 6 months; at the end of this period, her training would be completed and Mr. F. would be transfered to a new therapist. Mr. F.'s first therapist had terminated treatment with him when he left the area upon completion of his psychiatric training. Mr. F.'s mother died of a brain tumor during his adolescence, and since that time the patient had entertained fantasies that this tumor had resulted from the power of his angry thoughts entering her brain.

Mr. F. was a very bright man who had been hospitalized many times, first at age 19. His rich fantasy life frequently became crystallized in fixed, persecutory, and grandiose delusions with auditory hallucinations. During the hospitalization under discussion, Mr. F. had periods of agitated psychosis, wherein he became belligerently threatening and sexually provocative toward female staff members.

The patient very quickly became intensely involved with Dr. W. In the first session, he imagined his thoughts were entering her mind and achieving a state of harmonious, sexual union with her thoughts. Dr. W. found Mr. F. fascinating and frightening and early in the treatment had a dream of being physically attacked by him.

Over the first month of treatment, Mr. F. became preoccupied with what he imagined others were thinking about him. He often felt that people were laughing at him, sneering at him, or mocking him. In the course of recounting these experiences, Mr. F. commented, "I'm throwing things. . . . I'm throwing out ideas and thoughts. . . . They're kind of weapons. I need them. These ideas fit what's happening . . . not exactly, but someplace." On another occasion, after the patient used a tissue to wipe tears from his face, he threw bits of the wet tissue in the direction of the therapist.

Dr. W. was aware that she was very taken by what she felt was a strange and delicate perceptiveness demonstrated by Mr. F. and attempted to reciprocate this heightened state of awareness in her responsiveness to him. At the same time, her continuing fear of Mr. F.'s potential for violence caused the therapist to be anxious about being alone with him. She gradually became aware that her fear was in part a result of her own anxieties about conflicted wishes for romance with him.[1]

For the first two-and-a-half months of Dr. W.'s work with Mr. F. she allowed him to take the lead in initiating contact outside the therapy hours. When Dr. W. saw him in the ward hallway, she would nod to him only if he invited the action by saying hello or by nodding to her. This was in keeping with an effort on both the part of the patient and Dr. W. to keep the intense feelings of the individual therapy in the therapy hours.

One morning in the third month of treatment, the therapist saw Mr. F. in the hallway and said hello to him, even though he had not initiated contact with her. Later that morning, just before a patient-staff community meeting, Mr. F. abruptly appeared nose-to-nose with the therapist, and loudly accused her of biting her lip at him in an angry way. The patient made it clear that he felt rejected and hurt and demanded that the therapist meet with him *immediately* to talk about it. The therapist was frightened and felt unfairly intruded upon by the patient's unexpected reproach and demand. She reported feeling vaguely guilty about unknowingly having done something wrong. She was acutely aware of the public nature of the interchange and of the fact that it was impossible to think or to respond in a considered way under these circumstances. Dr. W. told the patient she would meet with him for about 15 minutes after the community meeting. Mr. F. stormed away without

---

[1]Such countertransference fears are an inevitable part of intensive psychotherapy with schizophrenic patients, and, as in this case, these feelings are not necessarily a reflection of unmanageable pathology on the part of the therapist. The capacity to allow oneself to be vulnerable to experiencing one's anxieties, conflicts, and fears is one facet of what is meant by being open to serving as a container for the patient's projective identifications. However, it is equally important to be able to gain awareness of and manage such feelings by integrating them with more mature, reality-based thoughts and self- and object-representations.

saying anything. At the patient-staff meeting, he stared at the therapist relentlessly. Dr. W. felt as if her face and lips were no longer under her control. Every facial position felt as if it might be interpreted in a way she had not intended. After the meeting, the therapist found Mr. F. at a desk with his face buried in his hands. He looked depressed and exhausted. He said that he did not want to meet with the therapist and would speak with her the following day at their regular appointment.

The clinical sequence just described involved difficulties frequently encountered in the course of inpatient psychotherapeutic work. First, there is the problem of conflicting subsystems within the hospital organization. The training subsystem placed value on training psychiatric residents even if it involved a limited inpatient training period. The treatment subsystem placed value upon the continuity of treatment and recognized the disruptive and destructive effects of premature termination. As a result of this conflict within the hospital social system, the patient and therapist found themselves confronted from the outset of the therapy by the paradox that the ward was designed to offer long-term, analytic treatment but that in some cases the individual therapy was of a sequential, short-term nature. The reality of this paradox created a setting in which it was extremely difficult to conduct intensive, analytically oriented therapy.

The clinical material also highlights a second feature of inpatient treatment that is frequently a problematic area: the added dimension of the work that results from the widened and less well-defined framework of individual psychotherapy, for example, patient and therapist attending ward meetings together. In the case described, the patient's poor impulse control and his feelings about the time limitation of his present and past therapies, further increased the likelihood that maintaining the boundaries of the treatment would be difficult.

The clinical situation that developed can be usefully understood in terms of a reverberating circuit of projective identifications. Mr. F. made clear that he experienced his own projective mental processes as acts of "throwing ideas and thoughts"—reified mental phenomena that could be thrown into other people, sometimes like weapons and sometimes like sexual organs. Similarly, Mr. F.'s throwing his tear-soaked bits of tissue toward the therapist dramatized the projective fantasy of ridding himself of his suffering and sadness, fragmenting it, and throwing it into the therapist—the fantasy component of projective identification.

Mr. F. initially attempted to protect himself and Dr. W. by denying his anger and by, in fantasy, converting his angry thoughts (destructive weapons) into sexual organs that could enter into the therapist and harmoniously fuse with her sexual-mental parts. The therapist partially shared in this mode of defense. She idealized the patient's pathology (seeing him as strangely and delicately perceptive) and attempted to create the illusion that she could understand him in a correspondingly hyperempathic way without his having to put his thoughts into words–the fantasy component of *the therapist's* projective identification. This state of shared denial and idealization was extremely fragile, as was reflected in the therapist's fears of being alone with Mr. F. and in Mr. F.'s paranoid symptomatology. However, while the end of the treatment seemed quite distant, this delicate state of shared defense could be maintained.

In the third month of therapy, under the growing pressure of her own guilt feelings about her deprivation of the patient (the upcoming termination of the treatment), as well as her own conflicts about boundaries (specifically, her anxiety associated with romantic fantasies), Dr. W. unilaterally introduced a breach in the framework of the treatment by saying hello to Mr. F. in the hallway. Mr. F. made it clear that he experienced the therapist's "hello" as an angry attack on himself. His hostile confrontation with the therapist represented his throwing back into her the fantasied mental contents that she had thrown into him, along with a large dose of his formerly disguised rage at her for offering him still another experience with inadequate and painful treatment.

Mr. F. had timed his confrontation with the therapist in such a way that his demand to meet with her was made just as another meeting was about to begin. The therapist was put in a position of being caught off-guard; she was made to feel helpless, unable to think clearly. In addition, she was made keenly aware of a sense of not being able to see something through with Mr. F. because of inadequate time. In this way, Mr. F. was inducing in the therapist feelings very similar to his own experience of having the therapist's feelings forced upon him at a time when, and place where, he could not possibly respond. The intensity of the patient's response was fueled by the more basic feeling that the time-limited therapy as a whole had failed to provide him with adequate time to think and talk about the feelings stirred up in him by the therapist in the course of the therapy. The patient's projective fantasy of angrily and destructively entering the therapist was symbolically enacted in the intrusive interpersonal interaction with the Dr. W. The patient's aggressive "assault" on the therapist is an example of the interpersonal medium by which feelings similar to one's own are induced in another in the course of projective identification.

Under the pressure of the intensity of this projective identification and of her own guilt feelings, the therapist introduced another breach in the preexisting framework of the treatment by offering to see the patient for a brief, extra meeting after the community meeting. Dr. W.'s feeling that she had lost control over her facial muscles was a further enactment of the now shared fantasy that the patient had entered into the therapist and was controlling her from within. The patient's fantasy of being able to enter into and omnipotently control the therapist was reinforced by the therapist's response, which was entirely congruent with the fantasy.

In spite of the gratification the patient derived from his angry and vengeful "control" of the therapist, the entire interchange had a draining and exhausting effect upon him, which is not surprising in light of the fact that he felt that he had succeeded in killing his mother through this kind of destructive, omnipotent control. His refusal to meet with the therapist after the community meeting and his statement that he would see her the next day at their regular appointment represented his own effort at directing the therapist back to the original framework of the therapy, which ultimately might offer him more help than would vengefully controlling her.

In summary, the clinical situation described can be understood as a sequence of projective identifications. The first of these involved the patient's attempt to defend himself against his own anger toward, and disappointment in, his therapist by: (1) denying, idealizing, and sexualizing his anger and in fantasy depositing these parts of himself in the therapist; and (2) exerting interpersonal pressure upon the therapist to share an illusion of harmonious and sexualized union. The therapist was unsuccessful in processing this projective identification; instead, she joined the patient in attempting to manage anger by means of denial and idealization.

As the shared system of defense became overtaxed by the reality of the approaching termination of treatment, the therapist initiated a second projective identification: she made efforts to rid herself of feelings of guilt over her deprivation of the patient and attempted reparation via a magical gift to the patient (her hello). However, the patient rebelled and responded to the greeting as an unconscious expression of the therapist's anger at the patient—an accurate insight on the part of the patient.

The patient then initiated a third projective identification, in which he imagined returning to the therapist her anger along with his formerly denied and sexualized anger at, and disappointment in, her. The therapist was exposed to intense interpersonal pressure to experience the painful helplessness that the patient had been living with from the beginning of the treatment. Dr. W. was only partially successful in managing this projective identification. She resorted to activity (the granting of a brief extra appointment) instead of insisting on reestablishing the original framework of the therapy. Finally, the patient unconsciously opted to help the therapist reestablish that framework by turning down the extra appointment and referring her to the regular appointment time on the following day.

CLINICAL VIGNETTE II

Chapter 2 discussed briefly an 18-year-old paranoid schizophrenic, L., who experienced his own self-destructiveness as so powerful that he had to protect his wishes for growth and treatment by attributing them to others. This was done via projective identifications in the course of which the patient (1) unconsciously fantasied ridding himself of these endangered thoughts and feelings, and (2) engaged in interactions with his parents and therapist that led them to feel totally responsible for his welfare and treatment.

> L. had always been out of step with other children his age, although he usually had some friends and did reasonably well in elementary school. Severe difficulties did not begin until the patient was 12, at which point he found that he could no longer organize his thoughts. Auditory hallucinations, looseness of associations, bizarre posturing and grimacing, and paranoid ideation did not begin until L.'s final year of high school.
>
> Despite frightening auditory hallucinations and the realization that his "mind wouldn't work like it used to," the patient insisted that he had no wish to see a psychiatrist and did so at the present time only under the threat of being thrown out of his parents' home. Previous therapists had either terminated treatment after one or two sessions or refused to even evaluate the patient, since he was unwilling to acknowledge any desire for therapy. In the present

therapy, the therapist accepted the fact that L. was unable to tolerate possessing wishes to change and grow and could only enter treatment if "forced to" under threat. The therapist repeatedly told L. that he did not have to like therapy or feel that it could help him. He just had to be there. The therapist did not attempt to offer him reasons for this stance, but simply stated it as a fact. In this way, the therapist made himself available to serve as a container for L.'s disowned wishes for treatment until the patient felt that he could allow such feelings to exist within himself alongside his self-destructive and self-hating feelings.

There were long periods in which the therapist felt like an unwanted and unneeded babysitter. He had grave doubts about whether his training was being put to any useful purpose by pressuring this adolescent boy, under threat of eviction from his home, to sit in a room with the therapist for an hour twice a week. In the beginning, the patient's father had to bring him to each session and stay in the waiting room in anticipation of his son's refusal to remain in the therapist's office. As time went on, L. came to the appointments on his own and was usually early. He began to act more relaxed with the therapist and talked almost exclusively about his hatred of his parents and the therapist for forcing therapy upon him. The developing tie with the therapist placed additional strain on the patient's need to disown his needs and wishes for growth, which included a wish to be able to love and be loved. As the strain of defending against fears of merger with the therapist mounted (about 9 months into the therapy), L. became more paranoid and fragmented, at one point smearing feces over the therapist's bathroom and then denying being in the building at the time it was done. In this way L. dramatized a projective fantasy of destructively forcing upon the therapist a debased, unwanted, and disowned part of himself.

Several months later, the therapist arranged for L. to be hospitalized. The therapist continued the individual therapy during the hospitalization, and a hospital psychiatrist was assigned to serve as administrator for the patient. L. was admitted to this ward about a month after another patient had eloped and committed suicide. In addition, an interim ward director had recently been appointed while a permanent director was being sought. The future of the existing therapy program of the ward was extremely uncertain, as was the future employment of the ward staff.

Although L. voluntarily admitted himself to this ward, he did so only after being ejected from his parents' home and being told that he would not be allowed to return until he received inpatient psychiatric treatment. Half an hour after signing in, L. announced that he hated "this dump" and wanted to leave. Shortly thereafter, he eloped from the ward. While he was gone, there was intense anxiety among the staff about the possibility of the patient's committing suicide, and there was an exchange of accusations about who was to blame. In particular, there was a rift between the male hospital psychiatrist and the nursing staff. L. returned 4 hours later in a drunken state, having stolen a bottle of whiskey from a neighborhood store.

The patient insisted that he had no wish for treatment and refused to attend all ward meetings and activities. Instead, he watched television and slept. Occasionally, L. would order the therapist or the ward staff to leave him alone and would say that all he wanted to do was to "get out of this prison." However, in the first couple of weeks, he did not *insist* that the therapist or ward staff leave him by himself and did not retreat to places where he knew they would not follow him, for example, into the bathroom.

L. eloped five more times over the first weeks of hospitalization because of different oversights on the part of the staff. The patient acted as if the staff were sadistic jailers for insisting upon offering psychiatric help when he did not want it. He "proved" by repeatedly eloping that they were not even capable of being competent jailers, much less functioning and valued psychiatric staff.

As L. demonstrated the ease with which he could "escape," his rebellious air gradually gave way to a profound withdrawal, not simply from other people but from external reality as a whole. He spent the majority of his time in deep sleep. He ceased complaining about his "imprisonment" which had previously been his one form of connectedness to the staff. He wore several layers of clothing, including four pairs of socks, two pairs of trousers, and three or four shirts under his jacket. The therapist met with L. daily and would sit with him as he slept. The patient did not acknowledge the therapist's presence. For part of this time the therapist talked about the loneliness and anger that he imagined L. was feeling. The therapist felt as if he were talking to a comatose person and felt foolish while he was doing so, but also felt bored for much of the time when he was silent.

The therapist brought some packaged cupcakes to one of the sessions and said that he knew that L. was not free to come and go as he pleased, and he might like these. (The patient had brought cupcakes to one of his outpatient sessions some months earlier.) The following day, the cupcake wrappers and a pile of crumbs were conspicuously displayed on L.'s bedstand. The patient rolled around in his bed, giving indications that he was not sleeping. Several days later, when the therapist entered the patient's room, the therapist found him lying in bed with his eyes open. The therapist handed L. two rolls of Lifesavers of different flavors. L. opened one of the rolls, ate a Lifesaver, and handed the therapist the other roll, saying, "Take these. I can't stand butterscotch."

In one of the therapy sessions in the second month of hospitalization, the patient handed the therapist a key to the ward and explained that about 10 days previously, one of the staff had left the key on a counter and that he had taken it and used it to elope on two occasions. He did not say why he had decided to return it and insisted that the key be given to a nurse and *not* to the hospital psychiatrist. After that, his elopements ceased and his withdrawal and bizarre behavior diminished. He began to talk more with the staff. Over the next several months he developed a very strong dislike for, and fear of, the hospital psychiatrist, while at the same time becoming adoring of several female nursing staff members.

In this clinical sequence, the patient relied heavily on projective identification as a defense and mode of object-relatedness. He imagined that the "good," growth-seeking part of himself was internally endangered and would be safer if he could deposit that part of himself into another person. Upon admission to the hospital and after psychotic decompensation, L.'s increasing sense of loss of control over his internal and external worlds caused him to redouble his efforts at disowning his responsibility for his own welfare and treatment.

In the hospital, L.'s refusal to attend meetings and his constant threats of elopement led the staff to view themselves as jailers dealing in punishment rather than as a psychiatric staff offering a psychotherapeutic program. More than that, the patient's repeated successful elopements had the effect of forcing upon the staff a view of themselves as floundering, disorganized, and incompetent. The patient's return to the "hated" hospital on his own after each elopement reflected his wish to *establish and maintain* a specific form of object-relatedness with the staff and not to end object-relatedness. The patient found it necessary to attack and devalue the treatment-seeking part of himself, which was in fantasy located in the staff. The condition of the social system of the hospital made it extremely difficult for the staff to successfully manage the feelings involved in this projective identification, since this entailed their containing for the patient his growth-seeking parts, which were then subjected to intense attack. Because of the recent suicide, the interim leadership, and the uncertainty about the future of the ward program, the staff was not able to feel confident that they could safely contain a growth-seeking part of a patient, especially when that containment was to be followed by intense devaluation of their ability to offer reliable and valuable treatment.

In an effort to rid themselves of the undermining effect of this patient, the staff was lax in their elopement precautions, thus tacitly permitting L. to repeatedly leave and potentially put himself in danger outside of the hospital. At the same time, the elopements were experienced by the staff as a defeat and as further evidence of their lack of competence and effectiveness. Therefore, when the patient returned, the staff was even less able to handle the projective identification under discussion.

The staff's leaving of a key to the ward in the open epitomized the conflicted behavior of the staff and powerfully reflected their ambivalence about living with the emotional stress of the feelings induced by this patient. Thus, the staff failed to adequately process the patient's projective identification, and instead acted upon their wishes to get rid of this undermining patient. The projective identification became progressively less adequate for L. as a mode of defense against anxieties about his own omnipotent self-destructiveness. As a result, his anxiety increased markedly and led to psychotic withdrawal.

The patient was extremely frightened of the bald statement of defeat embodied in the staff's leaving the key out. As with Mr. F., it is one thing to fantasize control over another person, and quite another to receive confirmation of the fantasy. Once the staff was felt to be controlled in reality by the patient's self-destructiveness, the patient could no longer make use of the staff as containers for his valued growth-seeking parts. At this point, L. despaired of being able to be helped by the staff and withdrew from people. Ties with the therapist were not entirely severed, and it was through this relationship that reparative efforts were made. These attempts at reparation were symbolized in the patient's surrendering the ward key to the therapist. L. then shifted to a different set of defenses, this time based on a split between a set of idealized object relationships and a set of devalued and fear-laden object relationships. The patient alternately viewed the therapist in an idealized and in a devalued way during this period. This new mode of defense and form of object-relatedness was in part modeled on the preexisting split that L. encountered within the social system of the hospital ward, the split between the male hospital psychiatrist and the predominantly female nursing staff.

L. developed a new set of projective identifications based on externalization of good qualities of the self into the nursing staff, and of bad qualities into the hospital psychiatrist. In this way, his growth-seeking parts and self-destructive parts were permitted to exist in tension with one another outside of himself and therefore were more subject to the internal controls of others, as well as those built into the social system. The movement toward these new externalizations does not represent significant working-through of the anxieties and fantasies involved in the original projective identification; rather, it represents an adaptation based on knowledge of the social system gleaned through the experience of incompletely processed projective identifications within that system.

FURTHER CLINICAL IMPLICATIONS

At this point several further comments will be offered about aspects of the application of the concept of projective identification that were not directly touched upon in the course of the preceding clinical discussions. Only a broad outline of the clinical material will be offered.

Group Projective Identifications

The clinical discussion thus far has focused on the ways in which staff–patient interactions can be understood in terms of projective identification. I would like to briefly discuss a group interaction on an inpatient ward from the same perspective.

It has become a cliché to say that a given member of a group, may voice or enact the feelings of the entire group, without being aware that he is doing so. But what is meant by that? How has the given group member ceased to speak or behave as an individual, and instead, come to function as the vehicle for the expression of collective feelings? I feel that when people talk in these terms, they are talking about projective identification in a group setting. For a great many reasons, usually having to do with the individual psychodynamics of the group members involved, a given set of feelings arising in a group setting is felt to be unacceptable or intolerable, and there is the wish on the part of many or all of the members of the group to get rid of these feelings. The group then polarizes into two partially separate psychological factions, with one part of the group functioning as the projector and the other part of the group, often a single person, functioning as the recipient. The projectors feel a bond with each other, since they all unconsciously imagine that they have rid themselves of an unwanted and unacceptable aspect of themselves. There is often a sense of virtuousness among those serving as projectors. In contrast, the recipient is viewed—and unconsciously experiences himself—as a container of the expelled, unacceptable feelings and attributes with which the group is collectively preoccupied. Pressure is exerted on the recipient to behave and experience himself only in a manner that is congruent with the shared projective fantasy.

> For instance, a great many members of the staff of a long-term analytically oriented ward were away on vacation at the same time. The patients were quite uniformly feeling neglected and uncared for. The community meetings for

several weeks were characterized by long periods of silence and then by rapidly diminishing attendance on the part of the patients. In a meeting during this period, one of the patients began to talk incessantly in a highly pressured, belligerent, controlling way that forcefully dominated the meeting. When the staff made an effort to allow time for other people to speak without being attacked by her, this patient bitterly accused the staff of "having it in for her." The other patients looked and felt victimized by this patient and were gratified by the attempts of the staff to defend them from this pushy, greedy, angry patient. Whenever it seemed likely that the belligerent patient would tire of controlling the meeting, one or the other of the patients would make an indirect reference to a situation in the past that this patient had found humiliating.

In this way, the unacceptable, demanding, and angry feelings of the group were imagined to reside solely in one member, who alone was insatiable and angrily controlling. This female patient experienced herself in congruence with the projection and enacted these feelings with fierce intensity. For her, there was the gratification of being not only allowed to, but invited to, enact feelings of frustration and deprivation. For the rest of the group there was the relief of feeling purged of these feelings; at the same time they unconsciously felt at one with the recipient when she expressed her feelings of neediness, neglect, and rejection in the face of the absence of a significant portion of the staff.

In addition, several of the staff members functioned as recipients of the protective, nurturing qualities of the internal good mother. This portion of the staff was seen as serving to safeguard each patient's internal good mother from the dangerously greedy child that the patient saw in himself. These staff members experienced themselves as nobly defending the helpless portion of the patient group. This role was eagerly accepted by these staff members because it helped to defend against their own irrational guilt feelings about abandoning the patients during summer vacations. Ideally, instead of having taken action as "protectors," the staff could have individually and collectively questioned why they felt such urgency to defend the "innocent" portion of the patient group.

Activity vs. Containment

An inpatient treatment setting offers an opportunity to take action. Of course, even in classical psychoanalysis, there is action other than thinking, talking, and feeling (for example, ending the session, shifting positions on the couch, payment of fees, etc.). However, there is a vast quantitative difference between this type of activity and the activity entailed in inpatient treatment, and this dimension of the therapeutic interaction must be considered a central feature of inpatient work.

The danger inherent in the easy access to action is the opportunity for the recipient to immediately translate the contents of the patient's projective identifications into action rather than containing the induced feelings and allowing time for the integration and understanding of the interactional process. The wish to get the patient to release the staff from pressure to contain feelings engendered in the course of projective identification is often rationalized in the name of getting the patient to "act appropriately."

On a psychiatric ward, the types of easily accessible action include telling a patient that one is too busy to talk, sending a patient to talk to another staff member, shaking hands with or hugging a patient, etc. Of course, none of these actions is necessarily in itself countertherapeutic but may be used as enactments of such defenses as denial, splitting, and projection in a way that would substitute for successful processing of a projective identification.

Members of the nursing staff often see themselves as the "doers" of the psychiatric ward, in contrast to the therapists, who are the "talkers." When this occurs, it is an extremely unfortunate development because it implies that when nurses are not doing (not acting), they are either being lazy and shirking their duty or pretending to be members of the talker group (the therapy group). The perceived role of any part of a therapeutic staff must include in its foundation the task of successfully containing and integrating projective identifications, predominantly by means of thinking and feeling (Lerner, 1979). The sorts of behavior (verbal interpretations, physical contact, cooperative task-oriented work, etc.) that would be used to make available to the patients the results of such psychological work would then vary according to the roles of the staff members and the individual psychological makeup of the given staff person and patient.

SUMMARY

After a brief review of several lines of thought related to analytic inpatient work, two examples were given of the way in which the concept of projective identification can be applied to interactions occurring in the course of inpatient psychiatric treatment. In the first example, conflict between treatment and training subsystems resulted in a form of stress within the individual therapy that the patient and therapist handled by means of a reverberating series of projective identifications. As is common in individual therapy conducted in an inpatient setting, features of the broadened framework of the individual therapy became the interpersonal arena for these projective identifications.

In the second example, conditions in the hospital powerfully influenced the way in which certain projective identifications were managed by the staff. The instability of the ward leadership and the uncertainty of the future of the ward program undermined the ability of the staff to adequately process the patient's fantasy of dumping wishes for growth into the staff. This was followed by an attack on the staff for unscuccessfully containing those disowned aspects of self.

Finally, two additional facets of inpatient work were commented upon from the perspective of projective identification: an aspect of group dynamics and the problem of easy access to action in inpatient work.

7
THE NATURE OF SCHIZOPHRENIC CONFLICT

HISTORICAL AND CONCEPTUAL FRAMEWORK

Beginning with Freud, analysts have been torn about whether schizophrenia can be understood in terms of conflicted psychological meanings or whether schizophrenia represents a disturbance on the level of the capacity to generate psychological meanings. The theory proposed in this chapter holds that an exclusive focus on either of these alternative levels is inadequate and that it is necessary to generate conceptualizations addressing the interplay between these levels, i.e., the level of psychological meanings and the level of the capacities generating these meanings, in order to develop a comprehensive psychoanalytic theory of schizophrenia.

This chapter discusses a psychoanalytic formulation in which schizophrenia is viewed as a form of psychopathology involving conflict between wishes to maintain a psychological state in which meaning can exist, and wishes to destroy meaning and thought and the capacity to think and to create experience. Moreover, the theory holds that not only are there wishes to destroy meaning, but that these wishes are enacted in the form of the schizophrenic's *actual attack* on his own capacities for attaching meaning to perception and his capacity to think about that which he perceives.

Freudian Theories

Freud struggled for over 40 years with the question of whether schizophrenia could be conceptualized in the same terms as the neuroses or whether a new set of terms would have to be developed. Between 1894 and 1937, Freud proposed three incomplete but overlapping theories of schizophrenia. The first theory (1894, 1895, 1896) viewed schizophrenia as an extreme form of conflict involving unacceptable wishes (later to be thought of as instinctual derivatives) and defenses against these wishes.[1] He viewed the differences between the psychoses and the neuroses solely as a difference in the type of defense employed and the degree to which the unacceptable idea and its associated affects are disowned. With these points of differentiation, the neuroses and psychoses could be conceptualized in identical terms.

The second theory was the most fragmentary of the three, consisting of little more than Freud's gnawing doubts that the strange behavior and ideation and the sharply different capacity for transference in schizophrenia could indeed be conceptualized purely in terms of conflict between unacceptable instinctual derivatives, defense, and compromise symptom formation. He made repeated reference to these doubts and to his suspicion that perhaps there existed a qualitative rather than a quantitative difference between schizophrenia and the neuroses. In 1896 he talked of an "alteration of the ego" that entailed a shift in the

[1]Freud's 1894 and 1896 papers dealt with the psychoses as a group and included both schizophrenia and paranoia. While Freud insisted that these two types of psychosis be viewed as separate clinical entities, he felt that—with the exception of the earlier fixation point in schizophrenia and the predominance of projection in paranoia—the two forms of psychopathology could be understood in terms of a single theory (Pao, 1973).

"thought-activity of the ego," although he did not specify what he had in mind by this alteration. The term *ego* seems to have been used here largely synonymously with "the person" and referred primarily to the way the person thinks. In 1911, Freud stated the hope that in the future it would be possible to delineate the "abnormal changes in the ego" that would distinguish the psychoses from the neuroses. In 1926, Freud again repeated his feeling that neuroses and psychoses are "intimately related," but added that they "differ in some decisive respect," the delineation of which was to remain an unmet goal of Freud's. In 1937 he returned to the idea of an alteration of the ego but again could not clarify the concept; nor could he distinguish between alterations of the ego in the psychoses and the defensive shifts in ego operations seen in the neuroses.

The third theory is the most comprehensive. It overlaps the other two in that it entails facets that highlight the continuity between the neuroses and schizophrenia and facets that have been understood by many analysts as inferring a theory specific to schizophrenia. The third theory (1911, 1914b, 1915c, 1924a, 1924b) centers on the concept of the "decathexis" of objects.[2] Freud conceptualized schizophrenia as entailing a fixation point in very early development (the autoerotic stage) with later regression to that stage precipitated by frustrating and conflicted object relations. Under conditions of conflict with objects, cathexis is withdrawn from both the conscious and unconscious representations of the object, and the displaced cathexis is shifted to the ego. In so doing, the schizophrenic not only severs his ties with or "disavows" (Freud, 1924b) external objects, but also abandons

---

[2]London (1973a) has detailed the shifts in Freud's use of the concept of decathexis and the corresponding alterations of Freud's model of schizophrenia. At times, Freud (1911, 1924a) used the term decathexis to refer primarily to social withdrawal as opposed to withdrawal of libidinal investment from object representations. In this sense, the third theory of schizophrenia represents a collection of theories grouped under the theme of psychological withdrawal.

psychological representations as a whole.[3] The schizophrenic's attempts to regain connection with his objects are only partially successful, and it is in these restitutive attempts that the schizophrenic symptomatology is generated.

Freud's third theory retains a conflict-and-defense format involving the wish to withdraw from objects (that is, to withdraw cathexis from conscious and unconscious representations) versus the wish to retain relatedness to objects (Pao, 1973). Freud conceived of both the neuroses and the psychoses as entailing a libidinal detachment from external objects. In the case of the neuroses, libidinal cathexes are displaced onto a less reality-based psychic representation of the object (Freud, 1914b), and in the case of schizophrenia, libidinal cathexis is displaced onto the ego. However, despite the similarity of libidinal decathexis of representations of external objects in the neuroses and psychoses, Freud was not at all certain that neurotic and schizophrenic conflict with reality and decathexis of object representations in schizophrenia and in the neuroses were comparable: "The most superficial reflection shows us how much more radically and profoundly this attempt at flight, this flight of the ego, is put into operation" in schizophrenia and the other narcissistic disorders (Freud, 1915c, p. 203).

The Specific Theory of Schizophrenia

Analytic thinking after Freud has continued to be divided on the question of whether schizophrenia and the neuroses can both be understood in terms of a single intrapsychic conflict-and-defense continuum, or whether it is necessary to develop terms specific to schizophrenia that are discontinuous with the para-

[3]Freud (1924a, 1924b) for a period entertained the idea that the neuroses and the psychoses could be differentiated on the basis of the former involving conflict between the ego and the id or superego, and the latter involving conflict between the ego and the external world. However, Freud (1927) later rejected this as a useful central point of differentiation.

meters of a neurotic model. These two orientations have been referred to respectively by London (1973a, 1973b) as the "unitary theory" and the "specific theory," and by Grotstein (1977a, 1977b) as the "conflict model" and the "ego defect model." Proponents of the unitary theory include Arlow and Brenner (1964, 1969), Pao (1973), and Kubie (1967), while those favoring a specific theory of schizophrenia include London (1973a, 1973b), Wexler (1971), and Freeman (1970).

London suggests that Freud's third theory is implicitly a theory of psychological defect or deficiency specific to schizophrenia. He feels that in Freud's theory of decathexis of the unconscious object representations, there is the notion of an "internal catastrophe" (Freud, 1911), that is, of psychological damage or deficiencies which consist of a basic disturbance of the capacity to create and sustain mental representations. This disturbance or "deficiency state" (see also Wexler, 1971) is on a level "superordinate to" that of psychological representations and intrapsychic motives; it exists on the level of the person's capacities to create representations and motives. From this persepective, Freud's third theory entails the notion that, to a large extent, the schizophrenic thinks and acts as he does because his psychological apparatus is defective on a level that transcends psychological meanings and, to that extent, the schizophrenic cannot be understood in terms of intrapsychic motives and meanings.

Bion's Theory of Attacks on Linkage

Bion (1959b, 1962a, 1962b) proposes a group of psychological functions (which together he calls "the alpha function") that convert sensory impressions into a form which can be psychologically recorded, organized, and remembered. These transformed sensory impressions are then available for conscious and unconscious thought. Sensory impressions that are not converted are treated as things in themselves, which are stored as "undigested facts" (as opposed to memories) incapable of linkage with one another. These undigested sensory impressions do not constitute experience, since there is no meaning attached to these impressions. Perception becomes meaningful experience only after the sensory impressions are transformed into symbols, which can be subjected to processes of conscious and unconscious thinking, for example, fantasy formation, dreaming, defensive operations, primary and secondary process thinking, and so on. If sensory impressions are not transformed into symbols, there can be no conscious and unconscious thoughts, no memories, and no capacity to learn from what one has perceived.

Undigested facts (sensory data unavailable for thinking) are dealt with by means of evacuation via projective identification in an effort to rid oneself of the build-up of "sensory accretions." Under conditions where there is a person available to serve as the recipient of this type of projective identification, the undigested facts can be processed by the recipient and made available for reinternalization as symbols with meaning. Bion offers a genetic hypothesis that the mother's processing of the infant's raw sensory data is the means by which the infant learns to process his own raw sensory data and thereby develops his own capacity for experience and thought. When the mother is unable or unwilling to serve as a container for this type of projective identification, the development of the capacity for experience and thought are disrupted.

Bion feels that projective identification is the principal form of linkage between mother and infant, and that the mother's refusal to accept and contain the infant's projective identifications is perceived as an attack on that linkage. The mother's refusal may take the form of a denial of the infant's feelings or perceptions, an enactment of induced feelings, an effort to evacuate the induced feelings via further projective identifications, and so on. The effect of the mother's refusal to contain the infant's projective identification is to strip the infant's thoughts and feelings of whatever meaning they had held previously. The linkage-attacking mother is then internalized and becomes the model for the infant's response to unacceptable reality wherein he attacks his own internal linkage processes, specifically his capacity to link perception with meaning (to create experience) and to link thoughts together. According to Bion, rather than developing an apparatus for thinking, the schizophrenic develops a hypertrophied "apparatus of projective identification."

It is here that I feel Bion's conclusions diverge from what has been clinically observed and are inconsistent with his conception of projective identification. He has described a setting in which there is an attack on the capacity to create experience and to think, and in particular an attack on the principal linkage between infant and mother—the mental capacities mediating projective identification. However, projective identification is not a physical "apparatus," but rather a set of fantasies and accompanying object relations; hence, an attack on thinking processes involving an attack on the capacity to fantasize and to establish connectedness with objects must necessarily interfere with, rather than enhance, the capacity for projective identification. In fact, as will be discussed later, as the capacity for thinking and experiencing is reduced, so is the capacity for projective identification; and as the schizophrenic approaches a state of nonexperience, there is a progressive reduction of fantasy activity of all types (including the type of projective fantasy central to projective identification) and a virtual absence of the type of interpersonal pressure characteristic of projective identification.

Grotstein (1977a, 1977b), in an unusually rich set of papers, fills in and extends Bion's work on schizophrenia. He views schizophrenic conflict and defense as originating in the infant's attempted adaptation to a psychological state of perpetual emergency resulting from either a constitutionally defective stimulus barrier or a constitutionally precocious sensitivity to perception. As a result of one or the other or both of these constitutional defects, a setting is created in which powerful destructive wishes and impulses are released prematurely. Hypertrophied and premature defenses are then brought into operation to deal with these powerful instinctual forces. These hypertrophied defenses represent the infant's desperate attempt to respond to the state of emergency described above.

Grotstein introduces the term "connative suppression" to describe the schizophrenic's attack on his own thought processes that not only destroys the capacity to transform sensory data into a form that can be endowed with meaning but also renders the schizophrenic unable to be curious about himself, much less to achieve any mastery over his own life. The schizophrenic lives in a "whirling maelstrom of disordered and chaotic non-thinking" (1977b, p. 434), which prevents him from thinking about what he feels and categorizing or even describing his experience. "He simply cannot know how he feels about anything. . . . In order to defend himself against pain, the schizophrenic attacks his own ability to feel" (1977b, p. 434). Grotstein stresses Bion's conception of the formation of "bizarre objects," which results from the projection of mutilated residues of "stillborn pre-thoughts." However, like Bion, he does not attempt to formulate the way in which a state of nonexperience is approximated, even though the rest of his formulation of schizophrenia (which centers on the idea of a destructive attack upon the capacity for experience and thought) would seem to demand it.

A COMPREHENSIVE VIEW OF SCHIZOPHRENIA

Freud's seminal ideas on schizophrenia and the analytic work which followed have led to an awareness of the need for a theory of schizophrenia that: (1) reflects the centrality of the psychological tension created by sets of feelings, ideas, wishes, fantasies, impulses which are felt to be incompatible, such as aggressive wishes toward an ambivalently loved object and fears and prohibitions about consciously owning such feelings; (2) reflects an understanding of the way in which specific adaptations to such tension (forms of defense and modes of object-relatedness) determine the form of symptomatology that results; (3) adequately accounts for the radical difference between schizophrenic and neurotic thought and behavior; and (4) addresses the relationship between the level of psychological representations, motivations, and meanings and the level of the capacities mediating the creation of psychological representations, motivations, and meanings.

A comprehensive theory of schizophrenia must address the interplay between the level of intrapsychic conflict and the level of the capacity for generating psychological meaning. In contrast to neurosis, schizophrenia does not involve psychological conflict in which incompatible meanings can coexist consciously or unconsciously in a state of tension. In schizophrenic conflict, there is an element of opposition of meanings in the sense of the opposition of wishes concerning experience, but the conflict is not played out on that plane alone. Rather, wishes for attack are acted on and do not remain simply thoughts or fantasies.[4] Neurotic conflict involves a tension between sets of meanings; schizophrenic conflict involves a tension between wishes to maintain a psychological state in which meaning can exist versus actual attacks on the capacities to create and maintain meaning.

The schizophrenic's various attempts to resolve this conflict results in the creation of types and degrees of states of nonthought and nonexperience which can be clinically differentiated. The idea of a phase of schizophrenia characterized by a state approximating nonexperience that is practically devoid of schizoid psychological processes differs significantly from the model of schizophrenia proposed by Bion and Grotstein and has important theoretical and clinical implications.

As has been discussed, Freud's conception of schizophrenia at times focused upon the level of conflicting psychological meanings and at other times emphasized the existence of a

---

[4]The idea of an attack on one's own psychological capacities for experience and thought ultimately refers to an unconscious act of limiting what one allows oneself to perceive and experience, and the ways one allows oneself to think.

specific "alteration of the ego," a change in the person's capacity for "thought-activity" that goes beyond shifts in psychological representations, levels of awareness, and psychological linkages. The model of schizophrenia that I propose takes as its focus the interplay between the level of psychological meanings and the level of the capacities involved in generating these meanings. The proposed theory attempts to delineate the relationship between the components of that duality, that is, the relationship between the state of psychological conflict and the alteration of the schizophrenic's capacity for generating meanings.

RESOLUTION OF SCHIZOPHRENIC CONFLICT

This section discusses four stages in the resolution of schizophrenic conflict, whereby the developmental gains achieved in the course of one stage lay the groundwork for the next. Each stage has its own characteristic modes of defense, symbolization, internalization, and communication, as well as its own level of object-relatedness and capacity for reality testing, and related ego functions. These four stages are: the stage of nonexperience; the stage of projective identification; the stage of psychotic experience; and the stage of symbolic thought.

STAGES OF RESOLUTION OF SCHIZOPHRENIC CONFLICT

I will now briefly present clinical material from an intensive psychotherapy of a schizophrenic patient. I will comment on the material specifically with regard to the ways in which it lends itself to being meaningfully organized around four different types of attempt at resolution of the schizophrenic conflict. For the sake of exposition, these stages will be described separately, although it must be emphasized that clinically pure forms of these types of attempted resolution are rarely encountered for extended periods of time.

The Stage of Nonexperience

Phil was 19 years old when he was admitted to a long-term, psychoanalytically oriented inpatient treatment program. Beginning when he was 15, Phil became progressively more silent, until at age 18 he became almost entirely mute.

About a year before he was hospitalized, he was found sleeping in the bedroom of a neighbor whom he hardly knew. Phil seemed unperturbed when awakened by the neighbor and escorted home. He was placed in special education classes in school, and sat compliantly through the school day as he was instructed to. His WAIS IQ fell from 105 to 55 during this period. When a group of girls told him to take his clothes off in the cafeteria during lunch hour, he did so—and seemed not to understand the ensuing commotion. Several months later, Phil showed no reaction to being hospitalized, even though this was the first time he had been separated from his parents in his life.

Although Phil was given a schedule of therapy appointments to keep in his room, he had to be reminded of his sessions each day. When he arrived at a therapy session, he would sit down and stretch his legs out. Occasionally he would rub his stomach, and when the appointment was after lunch he would burp and emit flatus. On warm days he would lie on the carpet and sleep. The sessions were experienced by the therapist as uneventful, but not oppressive. There was often a feeling of boredom, but not of painful boredom. Frequently, the therapist would attempt to look for meaning in the patient's sluglike demeanor and wondered if Phil were not attempting to communicate something about internal torpor or trying to make the therapist feel ineffectual or degraded. But these remained alternative theories for which the therapist could not develop much conviction. What was notable to the therapist was the absence of his own feelings of anger and frustration or of accompanying vengeful fantasies which he was accustomed to experiencing with a patient who was "resisting treatment." It was not interesting sitting with Phil, but it was not painful either. There was something so benign about this patient, such an absence of demandingness, such universal, indiscriminate obliviousness, that the therapist was not moved to feel anger toward him. The therapist did not feel his existence was being denied by Phil; rather, he felt he existed for Phil, but nothing more.

The therapist explained at the outset that he and Phil were meeting to talk and to think about whatever Phil was feeling or wanted to talk about. In retrospect, the recitation of this expectation to this patient seems quixotic and almost absurd. Phil seemed content to sit there as long as the therapist wanted him to do so. He never once introduced an unsolicited comment, question, or idea of any kind. When the therapist would ask a question that was in any way abstract ("What's new?" or "What did you think of the ward baseball game?"), Phil would either remain silent or shrug his shoulders. He would respond to very concrete questions, such as "How many hamburgers did you have for lunch?" or "Who won the baseball game that you saw on television?" But his replies would be incorrect as often as not.

Phil seemed devoid of curiosity or interest in anything, although he did seem to like watching television and preferred sports events to other programs. Also notable during this period, which lasted for about 8 months, was the absence of certain types of psychotic symptomatology. The patient did not appear to be hallucinating or to act in a paranoid or grandiose way; he seemed oriented to person and place (although he had very little sense of time); and there were no discernible delusions. In fact, there was no evidence of fantasy activity of any kind.

The phase of treatment just described is characteristic of the nonexperience stage of the resolution of schizophrenic conflict (Stage 1). What is central is the way in which all experience is emotionally equivalent: one thing is just as good or just as bad as anything else; all things, people, places, and behaviors are emotionally interchangeable. People, places, and objects are perceived, registered, and physically differentiated. For example, Phil could tell his house from his neighbor's house. However, since all things and places are interchangeable, in terms of their emotional significance, it made no difference to Phil whether he slept in his own house or in a bed in his neighbor's house. Since all behaviors are equivalent, requests that he undress in public were not seen as extraordinary. Nothing is extraordinary, because everything is of the same emotional value. For Phil objects were endlessly interchangeable, and this reflected a psychological state in which everything could be substituted for everything else, creating a situation analogous to a numerical system in which there are an infinite number of integers, but all are equal to one another in value. Addition, subtraction, and all other operations would be formally possible, but there would be no point in any of them, since you would always arrive at the same value with which you had begun.

Phil demonstrated no capacity for thinking about causes of events or about the meaning of behavior and showed no evidence of curiosity which might have suggested some interest in learning. There was no indication of any capacity for an original mental production of any kind. What he produced was on the level of physiological reflex activity: belching and producing flatus. It would be as absurd to infer psychological meanings from Phil's belches as it would be to read psychological meaning into a knee-jerk reflex. Interpretation of meaning in a meaningless field is a form of denial.

In the above description of the therapy, it was noted that the therapist experienced an absence of interpersonal pressure to think of himself or to behave in a particular way. The absence of pressure in itself could be viewed as a type of pressure, but this logic breaks down when one considers that a therapist in a room with a mannequin would either feel an absence of interpersonal pressure or defensively imagine some form of relatedness that might involve fantasied interpersonal pressure. Not all mental activity or feeling states of the therapist reflect the internal state of the patient. In attempting to determine the presence or absence of interpersonal pressure describable in terms of projective identification, the therapist's immediate and retrospective sense that he has been limited in the range of feelings, ideas, and self-images available to him is central. Interventions based on inferences made from an analysis of the therapist's intrapsychic state were not validated by the succeeding events of the therapy session or of following sessions. On this basis, it is possible to deduce the absence of defensive activity, communication, and object-relatedness based upon projective identification. This absence characterizes Stage 1.

It should be emphasized that although Phil's psychological state was devoid of the capacity to create meaning, there was no evidence that Phil's life felt meaningless or chaotic to him, and it would be inaccurate to attribute such subjective meaning to his life. The meaninglessness was not experienced because nothing was experienced: it was meaninglessness that did not feel meaningless, since there was no capacity to feel or to experience anything. The psychological-interpersonal characteristics of a patient in this stage should be contrasted with those of a patient in a state of catatonic withdrawal. The catatonic may at first glance appear similar to Phil in level of mental activity and capacity for experience; however, the catatonic very quickly (via his posture, muscle tension, and other nonverbal cues) communicates his powerful rage, as well as other facets of his system of meanings (Rosenfeld, 1952a).

One thing which is unmistakably clear when working with a

patient in Stage 1 is that even if one wanted to, one cannot force another person to think or attach meaning to perception. All that is possible is the attempt to create conditions for the reestablishment of the capacity for experience and thought. This primarily involves refraining from joining the patient in his attack upon experience and thought and making oneself available to serve as the recipient of the patient's projective identifications, if and when the patient chooses, however ambivalently, to enlist the therapist's help in achieving or regaining these capacities.

This view of the role of the therapist in the phase of nonexperience is based on an assumption that can be confirmed only retrospectively: the phase of nonexperience is not a totally inert one but instead represents a potentially alterable equilibrium reached in a battle between conflicting wishes. In Stage 1, the balance of forces has shifted so overwhelmingly to one side—to the side of hatred of reality and the wish for nonexperience—that there appears to be no conflict at all. The fact that consistent maintenance of a framework of therapy could eventually be noticed and responded to by the patient (as will be described in Stage 2) indicates that the "shutdown" of capacities for experience in Stage 1 could not have been a total one. What remains of the nucleus of the capacity for experience (including the system of meanings and wishes involved in the creation and maintenance of a state approximating nonexperience) remains so faintly present and heavily disguised as to be indiscernible for the period referred to as Stage 1.

In his efforts to create conditions in which the patient is likely to dare to think, the therapist must be certain that he himself is not attacking the potential for thought in the therapeutic setting in any of the following ways: (1) by attacking the stability, security, and reliability of the framework of the therapy by arriving late, changing appointment times, cancelling sessions, etc; (2) by denying an aspect of the reality of a field of nonexperience, for example, by interpreting meaning where there is none; (3) by attempting to escape from the patient's state of nonexperience through action, for example, by limiting the therapy to attempts at getting the patient to "act appropriately," which has the effect of encouraging action as a form of tension release rather than promoting the development of thought; or (4) by allowing his own unconscious hostility and fears of the patient's state of meaninglessness to be enacted by engaging in an "active" therapy, in which hostile, though only partially accurate, interpretations are made ("You are afraid to live life and do nothing but hide from it"), or by insistently demanding a kind of thought of which the patient is incapable (for example, by persistently asking the patient how he feels, or why he is doing what he is doing, which involve demands for causative thinking and the discerning of emotional experience).

It was stated earlier that, although the stage of nonexperience gives the appearance of being a nondynamic, nonconflictual field, there is evidence retrospectively that this is not the case. When the therapist is able to refrain from joining in the attack on thought and experience and has made himself open to receiving the patient's projective identifications, if and when they occur, the patient may begin to make tentative, highly ambivalent forays into the realm of experience. These initial forays, in which conflict is first evident, constitute the first projective identifications.

The Stage of Projective Identification

By the end of the fourth month of therapy, Phil was able to come to his daily therapy sessions on time without being reminded. In the eighth month, he began arriving late to almost every session, missing sessions altogether, arriving at the correct time on the wrong day, arriving just after the session time was over, etc. He always had an excuse: "I lost my schedule," or "I fell asleep and forgot to set the alarm." The therapist was annoyed by these hollow excuses but was at a loss to understand the changed behavior. The difficulty with the appointment times lasted for several months, during which time the therapist gradually began to count on the patient's being late and would allow hospital meetings to run over, thus arriving at his office a few minutes after the session was scheduled to begin. This generally "didn't matter" since the patient generally did not know about the therapist's lateness because he arrived even later, if at all. However, occasionally the patient would arrive on time and the therapist would arrive late. The therapist at these times reassured himself about his lateness by imagining that Phil was so "out of it" that he would not notice.

During this period, Phil initiated a form of interaction in which he would stare at the therapist and duplicate his every word and movement—his posture, placement of his hands and legs, facial expressions, intonation and tone of voice—and would repeat everything that the therapist said. This would go on for part or all of the sessions for several weeks. The effect of this was to make the therapist so acutely uncomfortable and aware of himself that nothing about what he said or the way he positioned himself felt natural. He felt that his body and speech were painfully and vulnerably exposed and had been to some extent conquered and taken control of by the patient. Phil's replication of the therapist's every motion and word had the effect of stripping his body and speech of the capacity to be experienced as aspects of himself and of their potential to communicate meaning. Instead, they were experienced by the therapist as foreign entities with which he was remotely connected, almost in the way one would operate a set of large, awkward, mechanical hands with one's own hands. The intense hostility of the patient's behavior stunned the therapist, and this further compounded the therapist's difficulty in reestablishing his equilibrium. The therapist felt estranged from himself and robbed of his sense of psychological room in which to think and observe.

The clinical material just presented represents the conflicted projective identifications that characterize the schizophrenic's first discernible forays into the realm of experience. The patient allowed himself to attribute meaning to the therapist and to the framework of the therapy by attacking the framework with lateness and missed sessions. At this stage, the fact that something has been experienced is signaled by the patient's attack on it and its meaning. The patient's projective identifications entailed the evocation in the therapist of a feeling that the therapy and its ground rules were meaningless, a sense that lateness and punctuality were equivalent, and that nothing about the therapy mattered. In this case, the therapist was not successful in processing the projective identifications. Rather than containing the patient's sense of anger and meaninglessness, he acted on the engendered feelings by being late for sessions. This represented confirmation for the patient that the therapist also felt that nothing mattered and that the potential for thought (the framework of the therapy) ought to be angrily attacked.

In the context of these interactions around lateness, the imitation of the therapist can be understood as a form of a "violent" projective identification. The term *violent projective identification* is used here to refer to a projective identification in which (1) the feelings of the projector are so intense and painful as to be felt by him to be violently self-destructive; (2) the projector fantasies ruthlessly and damagingly invading the recipient with the expelled aspect of himself; and (3) the interpersonal pressure exerted on the recipient is so forceful as to involve extreme (often traumatic) interpersonal intrusiveness—an intense form of impingement. In the projective identification involving the imitative attack on the therapist, the patient attempted not only to rid himself of his own feelings of deadness and meaninglessness but also angrily returned to the therapist the attack that the therapist had made on the patient and on the therapy through his lateness.

This violent projective identification is typical of the early part of Stage 2, in that it entails to almost equal degrees the patient's wish to destroy his own and the therapist's capacity for experience and thinking and the wish to make use of the therapist to create experience that can be available for thought. In the projective identification described, the capacity of the therapist to think and to experience his body and speech as his own were brought under hostile attack. In addition, as with all other projective identifications, this in part represents an effort to evacuate an aspect of oneself rather than experience it, live with it, and think about it. On the other hand, the act of inducing a congruent set of feelings in the therapist in the course of these projective identifications is also motivated by an effort to communicate an intolerable set of feelings (of meaninglessness and hostility) to the therapist in an effort to have him process the feelings and make them available to the patient in a form that could be thought about and lived with.

The form of object-relatedness involved in these projective identifications is quite different from that seen in Stage 1. The therapist in Stage 2 is perceived and experienced as a partially separate object into whom and from whom parts of the self can be transferred back and forth. The therapist is felt to be a dangerous threat to the patient's wishes for nonthought. For this reason, the therapist's capacity for thought is angrily attacked. At the same time, the therapist is viewed as a highly valued container for intolerable aspects of the self. These are meanings that a patient in Stage 1 would be incapable of experiencing. Projective identifications in Stage 2 reflect not only the patient's greater capacity for experience and for object-relatedness but also a capacity for sufficient linkage of thoughts to form projective and introjective fantasies.

The projective identifications at the beginning of Stage 2 deal almost exclusively with the patient's conflicting wishes and feelings concerning meaninglessness and nonexperience. In contrast to Stage 1, where there was meaninglessness and nonexperience without awareness, in Stage 2 there is awareness of meaninglessness that is felt to be so painful that it is immediately ejected in the form of projective identifications.

In Stage 2 projective identification is the predominant

defense, initially against feelings of internal meaninglessness, and later against feelings, perceptions, and thoughts that had formerly been so unbearable as to lead the schizophrenic to attack his own capacities for experience and for thought. The balance of forces in the schizophrenic conflict in Stage 2 has shifted toward wishes for experience and thought so that the schizophrenic now dares to transform perception into experience to the extent that some limited form of fantasy activity and attachment of meaning to objects can take place. However, the wish not to experience continues to be enacted: what is experienced is immediately expelled in the form of violent projective identifications.

The ferocity of the interpersonal attacks on thinking involved in these projective identifications accounts for much of the emotional strain involved in treating schizophrenics in this stage. For example, a 15-year-old schizophrenic relentlessly bombarded the therapist with hundreds of questions each session, to which the patient already knew the answers, "in order to be sure that the therapist was listening." However, this barrage had precisely the opposite effect. The therapist found himself unable to think or to listen to anything, since all of his energies were funneled into shielding himself from the onslaught of meaningless questions. Another patient repeated a demand again and again with a similar effect to that just described. In a group therapy context, Stage 2 attacks are directed at the capacity of the group to be a setting in which thought can occur. This can variously take the form of deafening banging of wooden objects on the legs of a chair, relentless reading of a book aloud during the group sessions, prevention of any discussion from occuring by endless breaches of group rules, etc. At times, the need and ability of a schizophrenic in Stage 2 to destroy the potential for thought in a group seems limitless.

For patients who are more verbal than Phil, the early part of Stage 2 is often characterized by exceedingly dry, repetitive accounts of both recent experiences and historical data. Hackneyed versions of psychoanalytic formulations are used whenever there may be the potential for thought. The therapist feels battered by the bleak monotony of the hours. All of this represents a projective identification of the patient's beginning experience of his meaningless, arid internal state.

Through the therapist's processing of the patient's projective identifications, the patient is able to experience a slightly wider range of feeling-states. These new feeling-states are in turn dealt with by further projective identifications. For Phil, this involved fears about his murderousness and the omnipotence of his thoughts, fears of being assaulted by the thoughts of others, and his fear and wish that the therapist depended for his life upon Phil. (The clinical manifestations of this type of projective identification are discussed in chapters 2, 3, and 6.) In the latter part of Stage 2, projective identification is less intensely ambivalent and is characterized by a greater effort to communicate unbearable feeling-states, and a decrease in the attempted destruction of the recipient's capacity for thought.

Stage of Psychotic Experience[5]

> In the second year of treatment, there were long periods during which Phil experienced painful blocking; he would look at the therapist as if stuggling to say something, then stop, then appear to be about to talk, and finally, in defeat, settle back into his chair or lie on the floor in silence. The therapist found it very difficult to watch Phil suffer this way. When Phil was blocked, the therapist sometimes repeated to him something Phil had said earlier: "It's hard to

[5]The term *psychosis* is used to refer to a state of psychological disorganization in which there is blurring of ego boundaries, disrupted ego functioning, especially in the areas of integration and reality testing, and ascendancy of primary process thinking. Schizophrenia is a concept referring to a type of personality system with a characteristic form of organization and development; psychosis on the other hand is a conceptualization of a psychological state which may be seen under certain conditions within the framework of any type of personality system.

think." Often, Phil would begin a sentence and then break it off in the middle. When asked what he was about to say, Phil said he did not know and shortly thereafter would be unable to remember having said anything.

At other times, Phil seemed frightened, disoriented, and confused. While in a state of confusion, Phil had no sense of how long he had been in the hospital, with whom he had just been a moment before, where he should be, or whether what he was hearing was really being said or was being imagined. He felt that any laughter was attacking mockery directed at him, that people or "forces" were going to kill him or wished him to kill himself, and that everyone could read his mind. He said that he desperately wanted to be able to talk, think, and remember but could not, and that frightened him terribly.

The week before the therapist's three-week summer vacation, Phil for the first time began to have auditory hallucinations, but he could not recognize the voices or understand what was being said because it sounded as if the voices were garbled, "as if they have been ground up in a meat grinder." While the therapist was away, the patient became almost entirely mute and paced back and forth in the ward hallway for hours at a time. When the therapist returned, Phil rapidly became less confused and stopped hallucinating, but could not describe what he had been through except to say that it was an "awful time" during which he had been very confused, had heard voices, and had not known what was happening to him.

There followed a period of months during which Phil spent part or all of his therapy sessions lying on the floor silently. He then began to smoke cigarettes during the sessions and would put his moistened fingers into the ash-filled tray and swallow some of the ashes. The therapist was startled by this and asked Phil what he was doing. Phil said that he did not know what smoking really was and that he felt that whatever part of him he had burnt up and flicked into the ashtray might be important. He thought he should eat the ashes, in order to give his body a chance to put the ashes back together into whatever they had been before and then return them to their necessary position in the body.

Shortly thereafter, Phil spent several weeks saying nothing, although he was apparently preoccupied with something. He frequently laughed deeply during these sessions; but when asked what he was laughing about; he said he did not know or had forgotten. Phil said that he sometimes laughed when he thought that the therapist had said something, but he immediately forgot what it was the therapist had said. He said that he enjoyed a laugh, but once he forgot what he was laughing at, he hated the feeling that he was laughing for no reason.

Before the second of the therapist's vacations (almost a year after the first), the patient pounded on his chair with his fist and said, "I know you've read a lot of books (pointing to the therapist's bookcase) and that you know a lot about psychiatry, but . . ." At this point, Phil fell silent and struggled for fifteen minutes to talk. He then forgot that he had been trying to say something. It was clear that the end of the sentence would have been something like: "but you don't know a damn thing about me and care even less!" Blocking became increasingly limited to situations like this one, where the ideas to be expressed were of a particularly charged, usually hostile nature.

This third stage is characterized by the schizophrenic's attack on his thoughts and feelings, primarily by blocking and fragmentation but also by projecting, introjecting, and bizarre distortions. Phil's blocking represented an achievement because he was beginning to have thoughts that did not have to be immediately ejected and processed by another person via projective identification. However, the blocking also represented the unresolved component of still-powerful wishes (that were enacted) to destroy his own capacity for thought and for experience.

Through experiencing successful containment of his projective identifications in Stage 2, the balance of forces in the schizophrenic conflict has shifted further toward the side of wishes to live with and experience perceptions and resultant thoughts and feelings. However, the aspects of experience that originally led to Phil's attack on his capacity to perceive, feel, and think, are still terrifying. Since the type of symbolization employed in Stage 3 is primarily that of symbolic equation (Segal, 1957), wherein the symbol (cigarette ashes) is treated as being the same as the thing it represents (a valued part of the body), thoughts and feelings have a vivid and immediate quality of being things and objects inside of oneself. Psychological processes are felt to be methods of physically handling these objects. For example, Phil's putting ashes into an ashtray represented a reification of projection, an enactment of a fantasied extrusion of a part of himself.

In the clinical material just presented, Phil can be seen to be containing his perceptions, thoughts, and feelings in a broader way than he had previously. This was reflected in his ability to experience very painful and frightening thoughts of people wishing him dead and attempting to kill him and in his feelings of loss before vacations. In Stage 2, the equivalent of such feelings would have been induced in other people and Phil would have felt much less of the pain of owning such feelings. However, the schizophrenic mode of reacting to painful experience—that of attacking his own mental functioning—is still present and is evidenced in Phil's fragmenting of perception and thought and his projection and then reintrojection of these fragments. Phil's auditory hallucinations, which were experienced as "ground up in a meat grinder," can be understood as projected reified representations of fragmented thoughts and feelings. The hypertrophy of processes of splitting, projection, introjection, and extreme distortion of representation mediates the process of psychological fragmentation. The outcome of this fragmentation is the creation of an internal and external world filled with bizarrely distorted remnants ("ashes") of reified representations of thoughts and feelings (Bion's "bizarre objects," 1956). When thoughts and feelings were particularly painful, as before the therapist's first summer vacation, attacks on the thinking process became escalated to the scale of a confusional state lasting weeks. Attack on the perceptual apparatus (as part of the attack on the capacity for experience) characteristically took the form of a breakdown of reality-testing capabilities, including the ability to orient himself (particularly to time and person), differentiate fantasy and reality, and organize elements of perception into a whole.

As is reflected in the clinical material, the latter part of Stage 3 is a transitional period during which the patient's psychotic experience continues, but in addition there is evidence of the beginning of a capacity to observe and to use words to represent, organize, think about, and communicate elements of psychotic experience. This was evident in Phil's ability to organize and put into words his fantasy that cigarette smoking involved the burning and loss of a part of himself that he hoped to retrieve by swallowing the ashes. This transitional phase of treatment stands out as a landmark in the development of the patient's ability to think and to talk.

The quality of object-relatedness in Stage 3 is quite different from what it had been in Stage 2. Here the therapist is valued, not simply as a partially separate container for Phil's projective identifications but increasingly as a separate person whose loss can be feared and to a small extent mourned. The feelings experienced by the therapist are also of a different quality from Stage 2. Now there is room for the therapist to respond empathically to the patient as opposed to having feeling-states forced upon him by the interpersonal interactions entailed in the patient's projective identifications. This is not to say that projective identification does not continue to be a very common and important mode of interaction in Stage 3; rather, Stage 3 represents a psychological–interpersonal field in which empathy can become equally important to the form of identification that the recipient engages in during projective identification. The therapeutic relationship in Stage 3 is in many ways comparable to the mother–child relationship described by Winnicott (1958) in the phase of development when the child learns to be alone in play while in the presence of the mother. In Stage 3, the patient struggles to contain his own experience in the presence of the therapist, with progressively less reliance on the therapist to serve as processer of the patient's thoughts and feelings.

In Stage 3, the patient's feeling states are more openly conflicted (that is, the strengths of opposing wishes in the schizophrenic conflict are more equal) than in previous stages. This is part of what contributes to the increased sense of the patient as alive and "human." In addition, the focal concern of the schizophrenic conflict has shifted from the issue of experience versus nonexperience, which was dominant in Stage 1 and to a lesser extent in Stage 2, to the issue of thought versus non-thought. Even during phases of fragmented thought in Stage 3, for example, during confusional states, the capacity for experience is retained (Phil's memory of the therapist's vacation as "an awful time").

At first glance it might appear paradoxical that a period of florid psychotic experience and symptomatology has been placed rather late in the stages of resolution of schizophrenic conflict. Clinically, one regularly finds that a rather long and often fairly quiet period of unacknowledged interpersonal pressure for compliance with unconscious projective fantasies is disrupted by the appearance of psychotic symptomatology and psychotic experience. A therapist often feels discouraged by this apparent setback in his work. Very frequently in the case of hospitalized patients, hospital staff and family members will pressure for the prescribing of antipsychotic medication at this point. However, the perspective of this chapter should help the therapist to understand that the apparent setback in treatment is more accurately conceptualized as an advance: the patient is attempting to experience what he perceives without destroying the capacity for experience as in Stage 1, and without immediately ejecting his thoughts and feelings interpersonally as in Stage 2. He is desperately attempting to live with his perceptions, experience, and primitive thoughts but can only do so by, in fantasy and in action, blocking, fragmenting, and bizarrely distorting what is experienced. If unmedicated, the patient is often found to be more alive and available for treatment than previously, even while floridly psychotic. The patient in Stage 3 comes to view the therapist as a person who may be a source of help with frightening experiences rather than a receptacle into which unwanted parts can be dumped.

A note of caution must be added here. A therapist who has offered successful containment of the patient's projective identifications in Stage 2 will sense the growth of the patient's ability to contain his own thoughts and feelings. The patient, with his broadened capacity for experience in Stage 3, dimly recognizes himself as the author and container of his terrifying feelings and thoughts. This development may lead to attempts to destroy himself and may take the form of decisive, and often successful, suicide attempts, or of violent assaults on others when projection is prominent. The suicide or violence is often unanticipated, since the therapist has reason to feel that the patient was getting better, which in an important sense he was. There is a very thin line to be walked in this phase of treatment between stifling the patient's opportunity for experience and running the risk of the patient's being overwhelmed by his experience and taking violent or suicidal action as a way of putting an end to that experience.

Stage of Symbolic Thought

Toward the end of the second year of therapy, Phil experienced a diminution of blocking, auditory hallucinations, paranoid and grandiose ideation, and confusional states. He had a renewed sense of the relative calm that had been characteristic of earlier phases of the treatment. He did not seem to be fighting with himself in a way that he had been when he was more symptomatic. One had the feeling that Phil was in a position to notice the external world more now if he so chose, although he seemed very reluctant to make that choice. In the therapy sessions, Phil often lay on the floor saying nothing and acting impatient to get the sessions over with. At times he would appear preoccupied or anxious about something and when asked about it, would say that he did not want to talk about it. On one occasion he said, "It's too secret . . . sacred . . . I don't know . . . I've just decided not to talk about it." Phil seemed to have choices now for the first time and would often choose not to think about his feelings in addition to not talking about them.

During this phase the treatment took on a definite pattern. There were occasional sessions during which Phil was able to think in a way that was distinctly new, but these sessions would be followed by weeks or months of silent torpor, or intensification of psychotic sympotomatology. In the sessions characterized by emergence of a new form of thought, Phil could not only think but also observe himself thinking. In fact, at the beginning the principal topic he thought about was his own thinking. Both he and the therapist were amazed and at times exhilarated when he thought about something in a way that reflected the fact that thoughts could be used to understand experience and were not simply seen as dangerous things which had to be either ejected or mutilated. And yet, his initial thoughts were expressions of his fears about the danger of his thinking. He talked about himself as stupid, dumb, and retarded and added, "If I ever was walking down the street and had an idea, someone would come along and punch me in the eye." The therapist understood this as a symbolic representation of Phil's conflicted feelings about his wish to attack his own capacity for thought. Later in the same session Phil thought clearly about what he would be giving up in the process of becoming a man and about the responsibilities and interpersonal problems with which he would have to struggle. He concluded that "by growing up, you're just asking for trouble."

Phil's new symbolic capacities were also reflected in

types of play that made their first appearance at this time. In one session, Phil pointed his finger at the therapist, pretending it was a gun, and commanded, "Hands in the air." The therapist raised his hands. Phil then ordered, "Don't say anything or even think anything. I mean *ever*!" What Phil had earlier expressed by means of the violent, imitative projective identification described in Stage 2, could now be symbolically presented in verbal and dramatic play. In both cases, he was attempting to deal with the perception of or memory of a thoughtless, wordless internal state, and a wish to rid himself of that state by forcing it into the therapist. In Stage 4, experience from a nonverbal phase can be reworked in this way using verbal and dramatic play symbols.

Phil attempted to disguise from himself and from the therapist his emerging capacity for symbolic thought. The long periods of torpor following "lucid" sessions had an exaggerated feel, as opposed to a primitive feel, as before. Phil's flatulence while lying on the office floor had a theatrically humorous effect, which could be joked about. In one of these sessions, the therapist said, "I think you're working very hard to convince me that you're stupid." Phil then asked, "What does stupid mean?" In part, Phil was asking what it meant when a person could not think, but primarily, he was "semi-deliberately" (Erikson, 1978) outdoing himself by saying that he was so stupid that he did not even know the meaning of the word.

Phil's talk and behavior indicated that he was noticing things in a different way and that principally what he was noticing was himself and his relations with other people. Phil began to comment on new articles of clothing worn by the therapist and went to the trouble of getting a suntan after noticing that the therapist had one. He did impersonations of the therapist for fellow patients. But most importantly, Phil indicated indirectly that he experienced his increased capacity for talking, thinking, and playing as making himself like the therapist.

As Phil began to talk and to think about his ideas and fantasies which earlier in this stage would have been kept secret, he regularly introduced methods of draining away the meaning of what he had just said. For instance, in one session he said that he spent a great deal of time imagining himself as a tyrannical director of the Kennedy Space Center. He then repeated the idea over and over in a singsong fashion. This type of repetition had the effect of reducing the idea to the level of a series of sounds without meaning, in the same way that one can drain the meaning from any word by repeating it again and again. At other times Phil would introduce an idea and then say nothing more about it. If the therapist were to inquire about the idea, Phil would act as if he had never said it. Frequently, Phil would say something but then elaborate upon it to the point of absurdity, so that the original idea was almost entirely lost. Of course, the singsong repetition, the disowning of an idea, and the absurd elaboration all had meaning in themselves, but these new meanings were serving to strip the original idea of its meaning.

As Phil was able to think about and remember his experiences, he began to feel worthless and defeated in the face of his many failures. In particular, there was a sense of despair about his inability to have any ideas about what he wanted to be, how he wanted to live, the kind of person he wished to become. He talked about how doctors were powerless to help a person if the brain had been "crushed," because "they wouldn't know what thoughts the brain should be thinking, even if they could put it together." Here Phil was using verbal symbols to represent his idea that therapy had put him back together to some extent, but it was an empty victory if he did not know what to think.

The theme of form without content appeared and reappeared during this phase of treatment. Phil talked about how he could not understand how people could remain married for years when they did not seem to have any affection for one another. In one of these sessions, Phil talked of his difficulty thinking: "I feel caught. I can ignore and push questions out of my mind about what kind of person I want to be. But that's being a coward and being stupid and not being responsible. Or I could let myself face questions, but when I do face questions, I don't know the answers." The therapist understood this as Phil's thinking about his capacity to avoid an idea by making himself unaware of it (by suppressing or repressing it). Phil was quite clear that thought can be ignored, but neither the thought itself nor the reality it represents is obliterated or changed in this process. Phil was also keenly aware that making oneself unaware of one's thoughts is a self-imposed form of limitation and stagnation that can be useful in one sense but dangerous in another.

The patient's ability to use verbal symbols and the level of object-relatedness reflected in the previous description was extremely fragile and highly susceptible to disruption by internal and external events. For example, separation from the therapist, errors on the part of the therapist, imagined betrayal on the part of the therapist (by beginning treatment with a new patient) were all at different times precipitants for regression to previous levels of dealing with schizophrenic conflict. Garbled auditory hallucinations, blocking, paranoid and grandiose ideation, delusions, and confusional states (Stage 3) were frequent occurrences as were periods of almost exclusive reliance on projective identification as a defense, mode communication, and type of object-relatedness (Stage 2). However, there was no evidence of re-emergence of a psychological state in which objects were interchangeable (Stage 1).

At one point during the session in which Phil's capacity for use of verbal symbols was relatively stable, he looked back over the course of his therapy: "I'm able to think now. I couldn't before. Now that I can think, I can know what I've been thinking about." There is implicit here the delineation of three different kinds of mental states. In the first he could not think at all ("I couldn't think before"). This would correspond to Stage 1. In the second, he felt that he had thoughts but could not think about them, make links between them, or be aware of them. This would correspond to Stages 2 and 3. In the third category, he could have thoughts that he could think about. This corresponds to Stage 4.

DISCUSSION

The theory of schizophrenic conflict offered in this chapter is similar to most psychoanalytic formulations of psychopathology in that it proposes a view of a person attempting to deal with different sets of perceptions, thoughts, and feelings which are experienced as meaningful, but which are felt to be so incompatible and mutually irreconcilable that one or more of the sets of meaning must be altered, displaced, disguised, disowned, removed from awareness, separated from affect, etc.

The theory of schizophrenic conflict presented, however, goes beyond this in that it proposes that that the schizophrenic's defensive efforts to deal with his thoughts, feelings, and perceptions can be exhausted. When this occurs, the sphere of conflict shifts from that of one in which meanings are rearranged in relation to one another to one in which the entire system of creating and dealing with meanings (the processes of perception, creation of experience, and thinking) becomes the center of the conflict. The schizophrenic unconsciously attacks his thoughts, feelings, and perceptions, which are felt to be an endless source of unmanageable pain and irresolvable conflict. Morever, he attacks his ability to create more painful experience. Aspects of this theory present great potential for reified and anthropomorphic thinking that could reduce this theory to the level of an attractive metaphor. However, this need not be the case if we are clear about what it is that we are talking about when we say that the schizophrenic attacks his own *capacity* for thoughts and perceptions as well as the thoughts and feelings that he does experience.

When I say the schizophrenic attacks his own capacity for thought and perception, I am not talking about a physical attack on an object, since thoughts, feelings, and perceptions are psychological phenomena and not physical objects. Rather, I am referring to the fact that a person can unconsciously prevent himself from directing attention to stimuli (internal and external), prohibit himself from organizing his perceptions, and prevent the attribution of feelings and meaning to sensory registrations.[6] As the person continues to limit himself in this way, potential experiences that could lead to the development of the capacity to more maturely live with one's perceptions, thoughts, and feelings are not allowed to be meaningfully registered, organized, and thought about. As a result, age-appropriate experiences are forever lost as nutriment for psychological growth. An apparently inert, but in reality dynamically alive, state of extreme psychological limitation develops that I have referred to as a state approximating nonexperience. Conflict over maintenance of this state is the core of the schizophrenic conflict. In the course of the resolution of the schizophrenic conflict, the patient allows progressively more attachment of meaning to his perceptions. However, almost immediately, the schizophrenic reinstates his prohibition against experience and thought by ejecting thoughts

[6]It is possible that in some cases this unconscious self-limitation may compound a constitutional limitation, for example, a limitation of the capacity to generate mental representations (London, 1973a, 1973b), or hereditary deficiencies in primary, autonomous ego functions (Hartmann, 1953). It is beyond the scope of this paper to address the question of the relative contribution of inborn psychological deficits of these types, psychological limitations that may be a response to early traumatic experiences, or such limitations that are reactive to a constitutional defect, e.g., a psychological response to an inadequate stimulus barrier (Grotstein, 1977a, 1977b). Schizophrenic conflict as presented in this paper is a second-order phenomenon which could result from one or a combination of these types of etiology.

interpersonally (Stage 2), blocking, fragmenting, and distorting thoughts (Stage 3), and still later, by stripping symbolic thought of meaning (Stage 4).

A second and related aspect of the theory of schizophrenic conflict is the nature of the fantasy activity involved. In the discussion of the stages of resolution of the schizophrenic conflict, thoughts and feelings were described as having been ejected (Stage 2), fragmented (Stage 3), or denuded (Stage 4). These conceptions reflect *in part* the patient's fantasies about his psychological experience. For example, the idea of interpersonal ejection of unacceptable thoughts or aspects of oneself represents the projective fantasy component of projective identification. An aspect of oneself is in fantasy put into another person; however, there is in addition to this fantasy, the reality of an interpersonal interaction that allows for feelings similar to one's own to be experienced and dealt with by another. Similarly, in Stages 3 and 4, there are fantasies of fragmenting ("ground-up" auditory hallucinations, and burnt-up parts of the self) and denuding (images of empty brains without thoughts and empty marriages without love, where only the form remains). However, as with projective identification, these fantasies are accompanied by activity.

The type of fantasy entailed in schizophrenic conflict, as described in this chapter, involves both symbolic representation of feelings, wishes, and thoughts and an associated set of actions (acts of self-limitation, described above) that result in changes beyond the symbolic sphere. Specifically, there are changes in the self (or "the person" to use Schafer's terminology, 1976) as opposed to changes in self-representation. The person's ability to perceive, to experience, and to think are changed, not simply his representation of himself perceiving, experiencing, and thinking.

The same class of fantasy is involved in projective identification; the projective fantasy in this process is linked with a form of action beyond a representational sphere, in which interpersonal pressure is brought to bear on a real external object not simply on a psychological representation of that external object. These types of fantasies are termed *actualization fantasies* in order to explicitly denote their association with a type of actualization that reaches beyond the symbolic, representational sphere. In the case of projective identification, the associated set of actions occurs in the interpersonal sphere of object relations; in the case of schizophrenic conflict, the actualization that accompanies the fantasy component occurs in the sphere of the person's capacities to generate experience and thought.

As previously noted, psychoanalytic theory contains very few conceptualizations that help to link the phenomena in the intrapsychic sphere (thoughts, feelings, and fantasies) with those in the interpersonal sphere (object relations with real external objects as opposed to psychological representations of objects). Projective identification is one such bridging concept. There is an equal paucity of analytic formulations that help to conceptualize the relationship between the psychological representational sphere (for example, thoughts and fantasies, self- and object-representations) and the person thinking and experiencing those thoughts, feelings, and fantasies. The person, including his capacity for perception, experience, and thinking, is not a fantasy and exists outside of the psychological sphere that these capacities help to create. His capacities for experience and thought exist in interaction with his own thoughts, feelings, representations, and fantasies.

Thoughts, feelings, perceptions, and experience are constructions or products. As with all products, there must exist a producer. In a psychological sphere, the products (thoughts, feelings, fantasies, etc.) exist in relation to the thinker and his capacities for feeling and thought (as opposed to the representation of the thinker). The nature of this relationship is central to an understanding of schizophrenic conflict as conceptualized in this paper and is addressed by the concept of actualization fantasy.

Until now, the notion of actualization fantasy, although not formulated as such, has been utilized principally in the concept of projective identification, to offer a way of thinking about the interface between the intrapsychic sphere and the interpersonal sphere. The present chapter conceptualizes schizophrenic conflict as involving a fantasy component (conflicted wishes concerning the destruction of thought that are represented in fantasy) in association with actual limitation, beyond a representational sphere, of one's capacities for experience and for thinking. The conceptualization of schizophrenic conflict in these terms represents an extension of the use of the concept of actualization fantasy to address the relationship between the sphere of psychological meanings (including wishes, motivations, feelings, fantasies, impulses, etc.) and the sphere of the person's capacities to generate psychological meanings.

SUMMARY

Schizophrenia is viewed as a form of psychopathology characterized by an intense conflict between wishes to maintain a psychological state in which meaning can exist and wishes to destroy all meaning and thought, as well as the capacity to create experience and to think. Moreover, there is an enactment of the latter set of wishes in the form of an actual attack on these capacities. Schizophrenic conflict differs from neurotic conflict in that the latter involves tension between coexisting sets of meanings that are felt to be incompatible, while the former involves a conflict between meaning and attack on meaning.

In schizophrenia, defensive efforts to deal with meaning can become exhausted, and when this occurs the conflict shifts from the sphere of psychological representations and meanings to the sphere of the person's capacities for generating such meanings. Four stages, or types of attempted resolution of the schizophrenic conflict, are presented: the stage of nonexperience, the stage of projective identification, the stage of psychotic experience, and the stage of symbolic thought. In each stage a different equilibrium is reached between wishes to allow meaning and thoughts to exist and wishes to destroy all meaning. In addition, each stage is characterized by a specific form of enactment *beyond the psychological representational sphere,* by which the schizophrenic unconsciously limits his own capacity to perceive, experience, and think.

The theory of schizophrenic conflict presented here represents an attempt to address the interface between the sphere of psychological meanings and representations (thoughts, motivations, and fantasies) and the sphere of the capacity to create meanings and representations. The concept of actualization fantasy is introduced in an effort to develop a bridging formulation that addresses the interplay between phenomena in these different spheres.

8
TREATMENT OF THE SCHIZOPHRENIC STATE OF NONEXPERIENCE

The ability of schizophrenic patients to manage feelings within the psychological sphere of representations is frequently exhausted and these patients then resort to psychological methods of dealing with their thoughts and feelings in primitive and pathological modes that reach beyond the sphere of psychological representation. It is these psychological modes, to be referred to as types of *actualization* of warded off emotional content, that will be the focus of the present chapter. Case material will be presented in order to explore the way in which psychological representations are actualized, both interpersonally and intrapersonally—that is, the way such events are played out, enacted, and made actual, both in relation to other people and in relation to the patient's own mental capacities. As the clinical material is presented, the rationale for both the content and the timing of interpretations and other forms of the therapist's processing of the clinical data will be formulated in terms of the framework of interpersonal and intrapersonal actualization. Also, within this framework, the concepts of transference and resistance will be expanded and formulated.

THE CONCEPT OF ACTUALIZATION

The sphere of psychological representations is made up of thoughts, feelings, fantasies, memories, perceptions, and so forth, often in diffuse, inchoate, and archaic forms. These thoughts, feelings, etc. are organized around sets of affectively charged self- and object-representations and constitute the realm of conscious and unconscious experience.

The nonrepresentational aspects of psychological life, that is, the sphere of psychological capacities, are in Freud's structural theory referred to as the id, ego, and superego functions and psychological structures. This sphere, which includes the capacity to perceive, to remember, to attach meaning to perception, to create, maintain, and process thoughts and feelings, exists independently of, but in direct relation to, the sphere of psychological representations. In fact, this sphere *produces* the thoughts, feelings, etc. of the representational sphere.

In addition to the sphere of mental capacities and that of psychological representations, a third sphere that will be considered is that of the people existing outside of oneself (as opposed to one's psychological representations of other people). Although other people can be given representation in a psychic representational sphere, they also exist in their own right outside of their depiction in that sphere.[1]

At times intentionally, but often unintentionally, the sphere of psychological representations has been treated by many analysts as the only reality suitable for analytic conceptualizations (Benedek, 1973; Ornston, 1978). As a result of the almost exclusive emphasis on defensive shifts within the intrapsychic sphere, analytic theory has developed very few concepts for examining the interplay between the different spheres of reality outlined above.

---

[1]The relationship between the sphere of psychological representations and one's physiological capacities (a fourth sphere of reality) is beyond the scope of this chapter.

For instance, the concept of identification, formulated in terms of modifications of one's self-representations in association with shifts in one's system of motives and patterns of behavior (Schafer, 1968) addresses the intrapsychic sphere exclusively. This type of formulation does not offer a framework to conceptualize either the impact of such a process on the recipient or the influence of the recipient's personality on the process of identification. The same is true for the concept of projection as traditionally formulated in terms of disavowal of an aspect of oneself in association with the attribution of the disowned qualities to an external object representation.

It is the premise of the present chapter that one cannot adequately understand many of the clinical phenomena encountered in the treatment of schizophrenia if the intrapsychic and interpersonal spheres and the sphere of mental capacities are each dealt with separately. Instead, the dynamic interplay among these spheres must be addressed and conceptualized. Projective identification is one of the few psychoanalytic concepts that accomplishes this task.

While projection can be described entirely in terms of shifts within the sphere of conscious and unconscious psychological representations, projective identification can only be described in terms of the psychology of two separate personality systems in relation to one another. The projective fantasy of one person does not remain simply an alteration in the representational sphere of that person. In projective identification there is an effort to *change the other person,* not simply one's view of that other person. This psychological-interpersonal process entails an effort to *actualize* the projective fantasy in the sphere of interpersonal reality.

Sandler (1976a, 1976b; Sandler & Sandler, 1978) uses the term actualization to mean "to make actual" or "to realize in action or fact." He feels that actualization is the process by which wish fulfillment in general takes place. In particular, he views dreams as entailing hallucinatory actualization, wherein symbolic representations of wishes are experienced as real. In the interpersonal sphere, Sandler discusses role actualization, wherein wished-for roles entailed in one's unconscious object representations are elicited from another person and in that sense made actual. My own use of the term also includes the idea of realization in action or fact, but differs from Sandler's in several significant ways.

I use the term actualization to refer specifically to the *transformation of an aspect of the representational sphere into a form that exists outside of the representational sphere,* that is, an enactment of a thought, feeling, or fantasy in the interpersonal sphere of real, other people, or a realization in the nonrepresentational sphere of one's psychological or physiological capacities.[2]

In this way the concept of actualization provides a unifying means of addressing interactions between the representational sphere and each of the other spheres.

In considering whether it makes sense to speak of transformations between a representational sphere of thoughts and feelings and a nonrepresentational sphere of psychological capacities, it should be borne in mind that the interplay between the representational and nonrepresentational spheres has become an established mode of thought in the field of psychosomatic medicine. For example, the mutual influence of sets of thoughts and feelings and the physiologic functioning of acid-secreting cells of the gastric mucosa has been demonstrated clinically and experimentally (e.g., Engel, Reichsman, & Segal, 1956; Kehoe & Ironside, 1963). Fantasies about the functioning of these cells (or

---

[2]I feel that one runs into difficulty if one speaks, as Sandler does, of psychological representations, e.g., in dreams or hallucinations, as actualizations of unconscious wishes. Hallucinations and dream representations, however real they may feel, are still thoughts, and no more realized in fact or action than the thought upon which the dream or hallucination was based (the latent thoughts and feelings). I therefore limit the use of the term actualization to phenomena wherein there is translation of events from the representational sphere into activity within a sphere outside of that person's thoughts and feelings. A further distinction between Sandler's work and my own is that he does not address the way in which actualization of psychological representations may involve the sphere of one's psychological capacities.

about something eating or burning one from within) are commonly elaborated secondarily, but this is not a necessary component of the interplay between the representational and physiologic (nonrepresentational) spheres. The term *interpersonal actualization* will be used in the present paper to refer to an analogous interplay between thoughts and feelings and nonrepresentational psychological capacities.

The State of Nonexperience

In the previous chapter, I proposed that schizophrenic conflict at its core involves a conflict between wishes to maintain a psychological state in which meanings can exist, and wishes to attack and destroy all meaning and ultimately to create a field of nonexperience. There is enactment of this latter set of wishes in the form of unconscious self-limitation of the capacities to create experience and to think. Nonexperience, a concept I have derived from Bion's work (1962b, 1967), refers to the failure to attach meaning to perception, leaving one with raw sensory data that are not experienced.[3] This conflict over whether to destroy meaning or to allow meaning to exist can be represented within the sphere of psychological representations. However, the central point here is that in schizophrenic conflict there is actualization of a set of wishes for the destruction of meaning that takes the form of an actual attack upon one's ability to create and maintain experience and thought, that is, an actual limitation of one's capacities to attach meaning to perception and to link thoughts in the process of thinking.

One cannot understand the nature of schizophrenic conflict

---

[3]Freud (1920) introduced a similar model when he proposed that traumatic flooding of the psyche with stimulation is dealt with by means of "an anticathexis . . . on a grand scale, for whose benefit all the other psychical systems are impoverished so that the remaining psychical functions are paralyzed or reduced" (p. 30).

if one blurs the distinction between symbolic representation of a wish as fulfilled (what Sandler misleadingly refers to as symbolic actualization) and enactment beyond that sphere, such that the nonrepresentational reality of the operation of one's mental capacities becomes modified. As will be described later, when wishes to destroy meaning predominate, objects are perceived, but almost nothing is experienced or attributed emotional significance. What is perceived remains undigested stimulation, things in themselves, raw sensory data without meaning. When perceptions cannot be experienced, one cannot learn.

Although I have found this state to be a common development in the course of schizophrenic regression, it has not been sufficiently discussed, in part because of the lack of a conceptual framework within which to formulate such a state. The often-used pejorative term *burnt-out schizophrenic* entails a recognition, but not an understanding, of the fact that chronic schizophrenics very commonly evidence a state of psychological inertness, which is referred to in the present paper as a state of nonexperience. Recently, analysts treating very regressed patients have begun to describe related states. Giovacchini (1979, 1980) has discussed primitive, nonideational mental states as "prementational," more phsysiologic than psychological.[4] Green (1975, 1977) and Donnet (Donnet & Green, 1973) have observed an inert psychotic state that they refer to as a "blank psychosis"; Grotstein (1979) refers to a similar phenomenon as a state of psychotic "invisibility" or "non-being." Lifton (1979) uses the

[4]Giovacchini (1980) views the "living vegetable"-like schizophrenic state as a reflection of early environmental failure resulting in a fixation in the prementational phase of development. Severe ego defects are felt to result when this early fixation is extensive. In contrast, I will discuss this nonexperiential state not in terms of fixation, regression, and ego deficit but in terms of early pathogenic interactions leading to a form of ego distortion in which ordinary defenses can be exhausted and superseded by a different form of defense, through which all meaning (even sensory-level meaning) is annihilated. Giovacchini is describing a fixation at sensory-level experience; I am discussing defensive nonexperience.

term "lifeless life," and R. D. Laing (1959) introduces the notion of "death-in-life" to describe similar schizophrenic phenomena.[5]

Understanding this state of nonexperience as an actualization of wishes to destroy one's capacity for experience and thought is quite a different formulation from one in which meanings are understood as having been rendered dynamically unconscious (by means of repression, splitting, denial, projection, displacement, etc.). All of these latter processes are types of rearrangement of meanings *within* the sphere of psychological representations and meanings. Repressed meanings (thoughts and feelings) are maintained unconsciously and are experienced in derivative form, in dreams, slips, symptoms, etc. A state of nonexperience, on the other hand, entails actual limitation of one's capacity to create and maintain meanings, not simply a disguising or removal from awareness of meanings that one has created and continues to maintain, albeit unconsciously.

As will be seen in the clinical presentation, the differences in the technical implications of these formulations are considerable. If one imagines that a set of meanings continues to be unconsciously maintained and understood by the patient, then one would address oneself to the patient's resistances to making himself aware of these meanings. However, if the therapist were to conceive of a set of meanings as not being allowed to exist, then he would address himself to the patient's need to limit his capacity for experience and for thought. It would also be recognized that the value of verbally interpreting this need would be limited until such time as sufficient symbolic representation of this limitation of capacity has been achieved. As will be discussed, one's notions of transference and resistance are significantly affected when one attempts to incorporate concepts of interpersonal and intrapersonal actualization into one's clinical thinking.

[5]Joyce McDougall (1974) presents a related finding from her psychoanalytic work with psychosomatic patients. She feels that these patients "foreclose" the psychological sphere of conscious and unconscious thoughts, feelings, and fantasies, and relegate potential experience to the realm of the body and its "psychosomatic creations."

CASE PRESENTATION

Robert was 19 when he was admitted to a long-term, analytically oriented hospital. He had experienced periods of hallucinations and paranoid delusions since early latency but had managed to keep those experiences a secret. He was born with a congenital degenerative disease of the retina (retinitis pigmentosa), but the condition was not diagnosed until he was 5. Until he was 12 years old he had no difficulty reading slightly enlarged print. By age 16, however, he had lost most of his sight. He could see only very large objects, which he visualized as shadowy forms with almost no definition or color. Mental representation continued to be predominantly visual even after the loss of his sight. When he was admitted to the hospital, he trembled continuously, and his eyes were rolled back in their sockets so that only the murky white sclerae were visible. He was experiencing "visual" hallucinations of thousands of spiders surrounding him, some of which were felt to be entering his throat and stinging and suffocating him from within.

Robert was the only child of a progressively decompensating, borderline schizophrenic mother and a father who withdrew emotionally from the family soon after the patient's birth.[6] The patient's mother had a pattern of becoming intensely involved with a particular image of herself and of living it out for an extended period of time, which might last from half a year to many years. She would then rapidly disengage herself from all her attachments and move on to another concept of herself in relation to a new set of people. Before marrying Robert's father, she had been married for about a year to a carnival parachute jumper and, soon after

[6]Extensive interviews were conducted with the patient's parents, as well as with other important figures in the patient's life. In the interest of confidentiality, it has been necessary to leave unclear the specific sources of information for aspects of the history.

that, to a nationally known professor of theoretical physics. The second marriage ended after four years when she became involved with the patient's father, a highly successful attorney. She seemed to move quite easily from one marriage to another in contrast to the extreme emotional distress suffered by her second husband. She seemed to immerse herself totally in someone's life and then suddenly shift the terms of her own life. It was not that the previous person was actively rejected; he simply did not have a place in her new set of terms. These terms, or meanings, were the product of an elaborate system of internal fantasy that kept Robert's mother only marginally in touch with reality. Certain people found the patient's mother magnetically attractive and afterwards referred to her with bitterness, almost as if she were a kind of witch with magically alluring powers that she used to hold them in her "spell."

The marriage to Robert's father was part of the mother's fantasy of "suburban life." They bought a home in the suburbs and two cars; she immersed herself in local women's activities and had a child (Robert) about a year and a half after the marriage. She continued breast-feeding for over a year, despite the fact that the patient's teeth, which appeared early, cut into her nipples, resulting in extremely painful nursing and intermittent infection. Although his withdrawal had begun earlier, following the birth, Robert's father became even less available and arranged to be away on business almost all of the time. The patient's mother labored to be a "model mother" and, reportedly with phenomenal energy, devoted herself entirely to this task for several years. In her words, she "threw herself into the baby" and attempted to anticipate his every desire. However, this was punctuated by periods of abrupt withdrawal, during which the mother became so involved in some activity (for instance, dance classes) that she sometimes did not return home for several days, leaving Robert, then 6 years old, in the house alone for some time. In addition, there were indications that the mother's ability to perceive and respond to the child realistically and empathically was quite limited: his visual defect had been subtly present for at least two years before a friend of the family pointed it out to the patient's mother, and medical studies were performed when Robert was 5. Robert's propensity as a small boy to kiss with his mouth open in a way that left a mass of saliva on the face of the person being kissed was seen as a French kiss and was felt to reflect premature, perverse sexuality. Robert's enthusiasm for a gift that the mother gave him resulted in feelings of extreme jealousy in the mother, which led her to view him as a "strangely materialistic child from the beginning."

The patient's first eight years were also characterized by intermittent bouts of depressive withdrawal on the mother's part, during which time she would cry for most of the day. During one of these periods, she became involved in a lesbian relationship with a woman who moved into their home and remained for a year. The relationship ended abruptly when the other other woman felt as if she were "drowning" and had handed over all capacity to think to Robert's mother. It was at the point of the breakup of this homosexual relationship that Robert's parents were divorced.

For the next ten years, Robert and his mother lived like transients, moving into the guest room of a friend's home or into a boarding house, remaining in that locale for a period of two to six months, and then moving to a similar setting in a new city or country. Sharing a single room for these years, the patient was present (until puberty) during his mother's sexual relations with men and with women.

Robert was rarely sent to school, even before the "wandering" began; by the time he was 18, he had attended only about four years of school, including tutoring. He did learn to read and in latency spent much of his time alone in his room with books. As the patient's eyesight began to fail, no instruction in mobility or braille or any other sort of training for the blind was sought.

At about age 9, Robert began to have visual hallucinations and delusions of spiders invading and suffocating him from inside his throat. He did not reveal these experiences to anyone. The patient was uniformly docile and compliant, never once inquiring into the reasons for all the moving. Beginning at about age 15, he spoke very little and when he did speak, it was in single words or short phrases. It appears that Robert had no sexual experience, including masturbation. His level of understanding of sex remained primitive and dominated by a cloacal fantasy of female anatomy.

Robert's father visited once or twice a year. When the patient was 18, his father noticed that Robert was acting in a subtly hostile way toward his mother. The patient was avoiding being with his mother and refused to have meals with her. This led his father to believe that Robert might still be "salvageable" and he proposed that Robert come to live with him. The patient's mother was growing tired of the burden of taking care of Robert, whose rapidly worsening blindness was increasingly difficult to deny. By this time, she had become deeply involved with religious missionary work and was living with Robert in a primitive town in Greece.

Robert went to live with his father (who never remarried) and was sent to a school for the blind. However, within a year after the move, the patient became floridly psychotic as described above, and was hospitalized. For three years, there was no contact (even by letter) between Robert and his mother. When he was 22, she visited him for a few days when her missionary work caused her to return to the United States.

COURSE OF THERAPY

First Clinical Phase

Robert was seen five times per week in individual psychotherapy. The initial months of therapy were marked by a steady deterioration of the patient's mental state. Initially, Robert was able to use single-word replies in response to the therapist's questions to communicate aspects of his experience of the psychological collapse that he was undergoing. Primarily, the patient felt under attack by spiders which were felt to have surrounded him, to have infested his food, and to have entered his throat to sting him to death and suffocate him from within. He reported delusions of being drowned by his hospital roommate, and of being blown apart by a bomb that had magically been placed inside of him. The only statement about any member of his family was about his father, who was said to "haunt" him. During these sessions, Robert rigidly sat in his chair, trembling, with his eyes either fixed on some corner of the ceiling or entirely rolled into the upper vault of his skull.

The patient became progressively more withdrawn and increasingly mute. This was accompanied by a diminution of anxiety and disappearance of manifest psychotic symptomatology. The therapist at times felt the anxiety of slipping into a "black hole" with the patient. For instance, the therapist observed himself insistently asking a series of questions about the patient's symptomatology in an effort to hold onto this disappearing thread of meaning and connectedness with the patient. However, verbal communication diminished and ultimately ceased, leaving the therapist with a sense of extreme disconnectedness from the patient.

By the fourth month of therapy, the sessions had become very still and would remain so for the succeeding nine or ten months. The desperateness of the attempts to hold onto the dwindling meaning and the vividness of the psychotic symptomatology were over. The absence of florid psychotic symptomatology did not feel to the therapist like a sign of progress, but neither did the therapist any longer feel the anxiety of slipping into something unknown and dangerous. There was a timeless quality to the therapy now that left the therapist devoid of a sense of urgency to do anything or to make anything in particular happen. The notions of cure or progress or improvement or of helping the patient were not a part of the therapist's emotional vocabulary in this period of therapy.

There were long hours of silence over these months which seemed neither interesting nor oppressive. During these stretches of time, the therapist observed the other person sitting in his office with him. He watched the patient use his cane to cross the room, lightly touch the foot of the chair with his cane, pivot on one foot and allow himself to drop like dead weight into the chair and sink into the cushion. Robert would then recover from his fall, adjust himself in the chair, and shift his gaze from one light bulb to the other in the room. He would then adjust the position of his cane next to him in his chair.

Robert, a tall, lanky adolescent with almost shoulder-length red hair, could not be identified as blind by his appearance. The therapist wondered about the patient's relatively healthy-looking eyes. What could the patient see of the therapist? How much fluctuation in visual capacity was there? The therapist noticed that the patient had dandruff in his scalp and that he had inch-long facial hair, not dense enough to constitute a beard. When it rained, the patient came to the office drenched and sat lifelessly in his chair in wet, clinging clothing. The therapist was not moved to take any action about this and was aware that he felt less compassion for Robert than he ordinarily felt under similar circumstances.

The patient's verbal productions were rare, and when

they did occur they were lifeless and mechanical. He answered questions and made statements, using short phrases that were highly stereotypic, usually repetitions of the ideas of the therapist or of other people. For instance, after the death of a senior member of the hospital staff, the therapist asked Robert how he had taken the news. The patient answered with a mechanical repetition of several of the words that other patients had used in the community meeting just prior to the session.

The patient demonstrated almost infinite compliance. Changes in appointment time, the therapist's vacations, changes in the therapy office, changes in roommates—all were absorbed without question and without observable change in the patient's behavior or demeanor. Again, when asked about his feelings concerning any of these events, the patient would either not reply or use the language of the questioner or of someone else in offering an answer, for example, "Did you feel angry about being pushed by Fred?" "Felt angry." However, the robotlike tone of the reply would leave one feeling that there was no genuine connection between the language used and the feeling-state that the words denoted. The therapist was not inclined to pursue such a reply with further questions, as he had done in the earliest months of treatment.

The patient slept for portions of the sessions, sometimes lying back in his chair, sometimes stretched out on the floor. After ten minutes or so the therapist would awaken the patient and ask him to remain awake for the rest of the session. The therapist found that he did not view Robert as an infant while he slept, as he often experienced other patients who slept at his feet during parts of their sessions. Rather, he found that he saw Robert as not fully human, as some type of creature whose behavior was not threatening, but not endearing either. When Robert came to the office in drenched clothing and shook the water from himself, it was very much like watching someone else's dog shaking water from its fur.

In contrast to his experience with other borderline and schizophrenic patients, the therapist noted that Robert showed no evidence of perceiving, or in any way responding to, the variety of conscious and unconscious wishes and needs that the therapist recognized or retrospectively came to recognize in himself (Boyer, 1978; Searles, 1975). It was not a feeling that Robert was withholding something; rather, it was a sense that the patient could not know what he himself was feeling (if anything) and therefore had no terms with which to respond to the therapist's emotional state.

This phase of therapy represents what I have termed *the phase of nonexperience.* It is characterized by a virtual absence of mental activity on the part of the patient and a corresponding absence of interpersonal meanings. The patient's total compliance and robotlike responses are modes of behavior reflecting an internal "shutdown" of attribution of meaning to perception and an almost total absence of thought. This state of nonexperience is recognizable in part by what is absent in the mental activity and behavior of the patient but, equally important, by what is absent in the therapist's response to the patient. The therapist does not feel repulsed, attracted, compassionate, parental, frustrated—as one might under similar circumstances with another patient—but instead merely notices and observes. The therapist's existence is not being actively denied; he is noticed and that is the extent of it.

In the therapy described, the therapist did not attempt to interpret the meaning of the patient's behavior. Robert's behavior was instead understood as an actual shutdown of the capacity to create experience and to think. Attempts at interpretation would have entailed denial on the part of the therapist of the way in which everything in the patient's life had been rendered meaningless. Although a phase of nonexperience superficially resembles a state of catatonia, the former is distinguished by the absence in the countertransference of the tension, rage, and fear that one experiences with a patient in catatonic withdrawal. Catatonia is a defense mustered against intensely affect-laden meanings. Schizophrenics in a phase of nonexperience have gone beyond defensive management of meanings; they have actualized wishes to destroy meaning by limiting their capacity to attach meaning to internal and external perception.

The phase of nonexperience is a psychological state in which wishes to destroy meaning are overwhelmingly ascendant and actualized in the form of the self-limitation of mental capacities. The therapist's tolerance of the long periods of silence and absence of discernible mental activity is not a reflection of a heroic capacity to endure psychological pain; rather, this phase of therapy, marked by its peculiar lack of interpersonal pressure of any kind, requires a specific form of psychological work on the therapist's part, which enables him to abstain from denial of what he is perceiving.

Despite the fact that ideas about the patient's apparent lack of mental activity were not communicated to the patient, the therapist's formulation *for himself* of an understanding of the features of this phase was an essential aspect of the treatment. He considered the unusual and often disconcerting impact of being with someone who had so completely succeeded in dealing with psychological pain by preventing anything or anyone to have meaning for him or to be thought about. The therapist's formulations were not in terms of the meanings that the patient was hiding from himself: they could not be because the patient had succeeded in denuding experience of meaning. If the patient had utilized repression, interpretations would have been formulated in terms of his opposition to awareness of meanings that continued to exist unconsciously. But that is not the case in a phase of nonexperience. The patient is not hiding something from himself; rather, he has limited his power to know and to think.

Previous meanings are not denied: they remain raw data, things in themselves that are not attributed emotional significance. Even the meaninglessness (perceived by the therapist) was not experienced by the patient; nothing was experienced, including the state of meaninglessness and nonthought.

Such silent interpretations, derived from the therapist's awareness of the nature of the countertransference, allowed the therapist to refrain from making interpretations that might have been appropriate in the case of a catatonic patient but countertherapeutic in the case of a schizophrenic in a phase of nonexperience. Repeated interpretations offered in a phase of nonexperience usually represent defensive activity on the part of the therapist that prevent him from being open to serving as a container for the patient's projective identifications if and when they begin to occur.

Deep schizophrenic withdrawal, similar to that described above, has until now been formulated largely in terms of regression in the transference to the earliest undifferentiated phase of human experience. Searles (1963) discusses types of transference symbiosis in which the patient treats the analyst not as a person or even as a part object but as an undifferentiated (but at some level external) "matrix," out of which his own ego may become differentiated (p. 663).

Margaret Little's (1958) discussion of the delusional transference in work with schizoid patients focuses upon the regression to an absolutely undifferentiated phase of development in which

> Subject and object, all feeling, thought, and movement, are experienced as the same thing. That is to say, there is only a *state of being* or of experiencing, and no sense of there being a *person;* e.g., there is only an anger, fear, love, movement. (p. 135)

Balint (1968) terms the most regressed phase of treatment the phase of "the harmonious interpenetrating mix-up" in which the therapist is treated as if he were an indestructible primary substance, like air:

> It is difficult to say whether the air in our guts is us or not us; and it does not even matter. We inhale the air, take out of it what we need, and after putting into it what we do not want to have, we exhale it and we do not care at all whether the air likes it or not. (p. 136)

Rosenfeld (1952b) similarly described the most deeply regressed phase of treatment of chronic schizophrenia as one in which the patient becomes "confused" with the therapist. This confusion is understood to be a result of powerful oral incorporative fantasies operating simultaneously with fantasies of entering inside the object.

Using different language and imagery, each of these analysts has attempted to describe the transference *experience* of a psychologically undifferentiated state. This is a markedly different type of formulation from the one being proposed in the present paper, which views the first clinical phase as being characterized by an almost total absence of experience of any kind, even devoid of the primitive experience of "basic unity" (Little, 1958).

Building upon the work of Bion (1959b, 1962b, 1967) and Grotstein (1977a, 1977b; Malin & Grotstein, 1966), I would suggest that the idea of transference repetition of the undifferentiated phase of development only partially accounts for the phenomena of the clinical phase of nonexperience. I understand this type of schizophrenic withdrawal as a revival of a *pathological* early state of partial differentiation from the mother in which the infant's projective identifications were inadequately contained by the mother. Ordinarily, where there is good-enough mothering, the infant develops the capacity to experience and contain his own thoughts and feelings by inducing corresponding feelings in the mother, who allows these feelings to "repose" (Bion, 1959b) in her. When the mother is capable of "reverie" (containment of the infant's projected feeling-state), a modified version of the original feeling is reinternalized by the infant in a form that can be attributed meaning (experienced) by him. In this way, the infant develops his own capacity to attach meaning to perception in a way that allows raw sensory data (internal and external) to be experienced.

When the mother is unable or unwilling to allow herself to be used as a container, whatever rudimentary meaning the infant's projected feeling-state has held is drained away by the mother's denial of the infant's feelings. For example, let us imagine an infant at a stage where he has begun to differentiate between outside and inside. Let us suppose he is in extreme discomfort because his diaper is wet and cold and causing his skin to burn. He kicks and screams under the pressure of the abrasive stimulation. At some point in the first months of life (I am intentionally leaving the timing of this event vague), the infant makes his first, very incomplete efforts at organizing his perceptions (raw sensory data) into the rudiments of an inchoate experience of fear, anger, and a sense of outrage that such a situation exists and is not being somehow immediately and magically rectified.

These elements of experience are communicated to the mother through the medium of the quality of the infant's cry, muscle tone, body movements, facial expression, feeding and excretory activity, breathing, etc. Let us also imagine that the mother of this infant is struggling with her own ambivalent feelings toward the infant, which feelings include unresolved, unconscious, murderous wishes. This mother might accurately deduce the physical source of the infant's discomfort but rigidly close herself to emotionally recognizing and rendering meaningful within herself the inchoate rudiments of the infant's feelings of anger, fear, and outrage.[7] This mother might efficiently, but mechanically, change the infant's diaper and fail to offer herself as a container in which the infant's primordial rage may be rendered meaningful in the context of her own personality

---

[7]When mothering is good-enough, this process of attribution of meaning to the infant's perceptions occurs unconsciously and unobtrusively. The mother's subsequent handling of the infant and his environment is the vehicle for the communication of the mother's unconscious equivalent of the therapist's accurate interpretation.

system. In this way, the infant's anger and fear are denied and returned to him (via the mother's rigid restriction of her attention to the mechanical task) stripped of meaning. What had formerly constituted the elements of the experience of pain-induced rage and fear is reduced to a signal for the initiation of mechanical activity. In this way the very earliest experience that the infant is able to generate is stripped of meaning.[8]

The mother's denial of the infant's projective identifications is experienced as an attack on the principal linkage between mother and infant (Bion, 1967). The linkage-attacking mother is internalized and serves as the model for the schizophrenic's defensive response to unacceptable reality. What begins as a transference repetition of a schizophrenic's experience with a linkage-attacking mother becomes less and less an interpersonal transference state as the schizophrenic actually carries out the attack on his own capacity for experience and generates a phase of nonexperience, in which even the meaninglessness itself and the psychological catastrophe it represents are not experienced. The transference repetition entails actualized progressive limitation of the capacity for experience, which eventually results in a state so devoid of meaning that it is questionable whether it can any longer be thought of as a transference phenomenon with all of the intrapsychic and interpersonal meanings that transference entails.

Second Clinical Phase

For almost a year, the sessions with Robert had settled into the routine that has been described and had become entirely predictable: there were long periods of silence; the

[8]Winnicott (1956) refers to the mother's capacity to contain the infant's projective identifications as her ability to "feel herself into the infant's place" (p. 304). The stripping of meaning is described by Winnicott: "After a persistence of failure of the external object the internal object fails to have the meaning to the infant, and then . . . the transitional object becomes meaningless too" (1951, p. 237).

patient shifted in his chair, took occasional naps on the floor of the office, or made brief statements of fact without elaboration or detectable fantasy content. The patient's blindness seemed so in keeping with the level of his capacity to make meaningful use of other forms of sensory perception that the therapist found himself no longer thinking of the patient as blind. Robert had a numbing effect on the therapist. Only in retrospect did the therapist realize how dull he had allowed his own powers of perception to become during the first year of work as a result of the almost total absence of discernible mental activity on the part of the patient.

Very slowly, over a period of several months, a series of changes occurred that were only subliminally perceptible to the therapist. The patient's personal hygiene began to deteriorate badly. Robert's hair became greasier and greasier; large, oily white flakes collected throughout his scalp and over his forehead. The therapist began to be aware that his office had taken on a foul odor, which he had been only dimly aware of previously but now felt assaulted by. He was struck by a powerful stench that wafted after the patient as the therapist followed him into the office at the beginning of each session. The therapist was stunned by all of this and wondered why he had not been alert to it before. He became quite anxious about how he was going to put an end to it. The therapist stared at Robert and noticed, not for the first time but in a decidedly different way, that Robert's face had a thin coating of dirt and grease on it. Flecks of food could be seen in the patient's inch-long facial hair. His clothes were covered with layers of caked-on food and stains, and some of the food would become dislodged or brushed off and left on the therapist's chair and carpet after each session. The therapist now viewed the chairs in his office as very much his own property that was being abused by the patient. The therapist had never felt such keen feelings of ownership of the furniture in his office. As Robert leaned back in his chair, the therapist's muscles tightened as he watched the patient grind his filthy hair into the cushion that made up the back of the chair. The therapist felt a great urgency to correct this situation and asked the patient why his hygiene had deteriorated so dramatically. The patient did not reply. This lack of response was experienced by the therapist as defiance, whereas no such impression had existed earlier when the patient did not answer questions.

The therapist was aware that the patient's behavior was leading the therapist to feel out of control. He experienced an intense need to get the patient to stop doing whatever it was that was having this effect upon the therapist; it was extremely difficult being with the patient while this condition persisted. The therapist was not able to be clear with himself about the precise nature of the interpersonal phenomenon in which he was participating and into which he was being further drawn. In the past, he had found some relief from similar interpersonal tension by analyzing such situations in terms of projective identification. However, at present, such attempts at understanding the situation seemed overly intellectual and were felt to be of limited value in helping the therapist to extricate himself from the maelstrom into which he felt himself being drawn.

The patient's odor worsened and the therapist became even further enraged when he found that the cushion on the patient's chair had absorbed the patient's odor and continued to emit that stench even in Robert's absence. The therapist washed the pillow several times over the next weeks with different types of solvent, to no avail. The patient's odor became a preoccupation for the therapist, who found himself changing seats in restaurants and movie theaters in order to avoid people with odors that reminded him of Robert. Initially, Robert resisted every pressure placed upon him by the hospital staff to bathe. Finally, he consented to shower daily but did so in such a perfunctory manner that the improvement was minimal.

The therapist experienced the patient's odor as ever-accumulating and now found the silence of the sessions to be tension-filled struggles. The therapist seethed as he watched the patient sitting in "his" chair and felt that the patient, with his ability not to think, was far better equipped for this kind of struggle by silence than was the therapist. The patient's blindness was imagined to be an additional aid in insulating him from the anger the therapist experienced as he scrutinized the patient's food-flecked face and grease-laden hair. During one of these sessions, a loud ambulance or police-car siren was heard, and the patient, not unexpectedly, said, "A siren." He then chuckled and added, "They're coming to get you, to lock you up." After along pause, he added, "You're surrounded." This was the first instance of verbalized fantasy activity since the early psychotic symptomatology. The therapist felt momentary relief from the pressure of the interpersonal struggle and said, "You mean invaded, don't you?" The patient smiled but did not reply. Over the next year, each time a siren was heard (which was at least once a week), the patient would say, "They're gonna come in and get you."

With the help of the patient's verbalized fantasy material and in the atmosphere of the somewhat lowered interpersonal tension, the therapist could begin to understand more fully aspects of the nature and meaning of the interaction centering on the patient's odor. The therapist was able, for the first time, to free himself from the rigidly limited range of thoughts, feelings, and self- and object-representations with which he had been operating for some time. Gradually, as will be described below, the therapist was able to more accurately formulate the meaning of what had been transpiring between himself and the patient. As this occurred he found that Robert's odor no longer had the same powerfully engaging and infuriating impact on him. The odor was still unpleasant, but the therapist no longer felt he *had to* escape from it.

Over the next two or three months, the patient's personal hygiene improved, more by his losing interest in being filthy than by his acquisition of new skills. Also during this period, further fantasy material consistently reflected the centrality of the theme of invasive, suffocating attack. The early hallucinations of spiders invading and suffocating the patient from within his throat,[9] as well as the delusional fear of being drowned by his roommate and "haunted" by his father, could all now be seen as a vivid confirmation of the emerging view of the patient as consumed by the sense of himself as invaded and suffused.

The therapist came to view the phase of therapy just described as having begun with the rapid deterioration of Robert's personal hygiene to the point that his odor became a vehicle for the interpersonal actualization of an unconscious fantasy (that is, a vehicle for projective identification). The fantasy involved the idea of ejecting into the therapist the feeling of being permeated by, and suffocatingly intertwined with, an-

---

[9]Freud (reported by Abraham, 1922) was the first of many analytsts interested in spider symbolism to draw attention to the biological fact that female spiders during sexual union frequently kill the male by forcefully fastening him in her grip and sucking his body contents until only a lifeless shell remains. In the analytic literature, the spider has been understood to symbolize the frightening, castrating, phallic mother (Abraham, 1922) and, in particular, the danger of loving and being loved by the mother in the oral phase of development (R. Little, 1966, 1967; Sterba, 1950). In what is to date the most comprehensive psychoanalytic study of spider symbolism, Graber (1925) states that in mythology, legends, dreams, and symptomatology, the spider symbolizes both death and sexuality, which are equated with one another. The death that the spider brings is the "death of love." In the case under discussion, the spider is understood to represent a particular facet of the danger inherent in the earliest form of relatedness to the mother, namely, the danger involved in symbiotic union. The spiders surrounding the patient and suffocatingly entering his throat represent the mother of late symbiosis, who is alluring and yet threatening to haunt and suffuse the patient (or be suffused by him) to the point that the two dissolve into one another—thus annihilating the patient as a separate entity.

other person. The therapist was pressured to experience himself as genuinely contaminated and suffused by the invasive quality of the patient, symbolized by his odor. Under this pressure, the therapist became fearful that his possessions (with which he had become closely identified) had been permanently and destructively infiltrated by the patient. The therapist was unable to successfully contain and integrate the induced feelings and instead felt overwhelmed by these feelings and pressured to escape from them. In the patient's mind, it was not enough for the therapist to understand what it is *like* to be suffused. The primitive wish of the patient was for the therapist *to be the patient himself, suffused with the object.* The patient's omnipotent fantasy was one of inhabiting and controlling the therapist and in this way being *known* by the therapist. In addition, there is the hope that the therapist might also be able to contain a hated and destructive part of the patient.

Nonverbal transference enactments in conjunction with the associated countertransference states were important sources of data for the formulation described. In a predominantly nonverbal phase of therapy, one must necessarily rely heavily on such data. Interactions and communications in later, more verbally symbolic stages of therapy provide data that can confirm or invalidate the earlier formulations. For instance, in the third year of therapy, Robert experienced a circumscribed psychotic regression. By this time, there had been significant advances in self–object differentiation and in the capacity to use words to represent ideas and feelings. Robert was at that point able to symbolize in words aspects of the state of symbiotic fusion that had been enacted interpersonally in the odor projective identification.

> During the psychotic regression in the third year, Robert began to feel that the therapist was "haunting" him. He was having auditory hallucinations of the therapist's voice, which were experienced as intertwined and "blended" with the sound and feel of his own thoughts. At moments of greater differentiation, he experienced feelings of anger at

the therapist for "haunting" him. The patient vomited after four of these therapy sessions. As Robert regressed further, he said that he felt that his head had been chopped off ("like an atom being split") and that his "haunted head" then felt like it was haunting the therapist.

Robert at first reported that the therapist was able to see only out of the patient's eyes. Then the therapist became indistinguishable from the split-off haunted head. The patient's rebellion against being suffused or haunted was clearly symbolized in his fantasy of splitting off and projecting the haunted aspect of himself. Moreover, the patient fantasied that the suffused self (the haunted head) was deposited into the therapist in a way that at first controlled him and then merged with him.

In the course of discussing these feelings and ideas with the patient, the therapist commented that almost identical feelings had been present earlier in the therapy when the patient's odor had filled the office. The patient indicated that he had felt something very similar during that period but that he "wasn't a person then." Now he feels more like a person but he is "afraid of becoming nobody if [his] head is chopped off too many times and haunts too many people." Robert was in this way verbalizing his fears of losing himself via fantasied ejection of his suffused self into the therapist. There is also a reference here to the fear that he will again begin to become nonexistent in order to escape conflicted feelings related to being suffused.

In the third year of therapy, such fears could be represented in words, whereas previously such ideas could only be enacted interpersonally in the form of projective identification (the second clinical phase) or intrapersonally by limitation of his mental capacities (the first phase of therapy).

Third Clinical Phase

In the middle of the second year of therapy, the patient evidenced signs of mounting anxiety that quickly developed into a state of paralyzing fear. When asked about it, he would simply say that the cause was "from being with you." Robert again began to appear at his sessions trembling, with his eyes rolled back into their sockets. When the therapist inquired further into the basis of the patient's extreme fearfulness, Robert appeared to be attempting to answer, but could not do so. At times, he could begin a sentence but would almost immediately become blocked. The patient frequently turned his head rapidly in one direction or another in what the therapist inferred to be a response to visual hallucinations. (This was later confirmed.) These hallucinations were later called "black-and-white forms" and consisted of a cluster of tormenting shapes that the patient felt were individually living remnants of a shattered face.

As Robert's blocking continued, his failed attempts at speech appeared to become more and more painful. For the first time in 18 months, the patient was experiencing anxiety. Not only was he now able to observe and attach words to this feeling-state, he could also begin to conceive of feelings as responses to other people. The therapist viewed this development in the context of a progression in the transference from an initial phase of defensive nonexperience, to a symbiotic phase characterized by management of feelings through projective identification, and finally to the present capacity to experience and observe his anxiety about being with the therapist. On the basis of this understanding of the first 18 months of work, over the course of several weeks, the therapist offered the interpretation that the patient had begun to allow himself to think and to experience feelings. The therapist indicated in short, simple sentences that he thought that these activities (thinking and feeling) made the patient vulnerable to pain from which he had formerly fled by means of attempting to prevent himself from experiencing anything at all. Now that Robert was daring to have his own thoughts and feelings, he was finding it extremely frightening being with the therapist.

Robert became visibly calmer in the course of each of these sessions in which a part of the interpretation was offered: the trembling steadily declined, his eyes returned to a flexible, forward gaze, his muscle tension decreased markedly, and his blocked attempts at speech ceased. There was a definite quality of childlike softness about the patient, which the therapist had not been previously aware of. As he offered these comments and observed the patient's response to them, the therapist experienced rather intense feelings of pleasurable closeness and maternal protectiveness. For the first time, the therapist had conscious fantasies of "curing" the patient. He imagined at times during this period that when the patient did begin to speak in a more sustained way, he would talk with a voice that sounded just like that of the therapist.

During one of these anxious sessions, quite out of the blue, the patient said in a thin and muffled voice, "Your voice sounds like me." He would not elaborate. The therapist was stunned by the fact that Robert seemed also to be thinking about the relationship between the sound of his own voice and that of the therapist's. There followed long periods of silence and then, again unexpectedly, the patient said, "Are you crazy?" (Another patient had accused the therapist of being crazy in a community meeting that Robert had attended earlier that same day.) As the therapist thought about this, he said, "So you think I might be crazy." The patient smiled one of his rare but warm smiles and said, "Only when you talk." When asked more about the therapist's craziness, Robert said, "Your crazy talk is not as crazy as me." It became clear over the next several sessions that the patient took great pleasure in the idea of the therapist being crazy in his "own special way," and that the sound of the therapist's voice was equated with a kind of craziness that had a profoundly calming effect upon the patient.

Over the next few weeks, a pattern developed, wherein Robert became extremely frightened between sessions and would call the therapist on the phone as often as half a dozen times a day, including on weekends. He would say nothing (not even "Hello") and would wait for the therapist to speak. When the therapist did talk, the patient's anxiety immediately diminished. This type of interaction was repeated within the therapy hours as well, where it became clear that the therapist's speech (as opposed to other forms of evidence of his presence) was experienced by Robert as powerfully soothing.

The therapist reviewed with the patient his observations of the patient's response to the interpretation, including the calming effect of the sound of the therapist's talk and the pleasure Robert took in the therapist's "special kind of craziness." The therapist then said that he thought Robert felt that the therapist could rid Robert of his craziness by transporting Robert's painful thoughts into the therapist's mind, where he would then render them harmless by putting them into words. The patient immediately responded, "Well, can't you?" The therapist laughed and said, "Perhaps you and I might sometimes wish that were so. Fortunately or unfortunately, we each have our own thoughts and feelings that we have to live with."

Following this session, the phone calls continued but were markedly changed in quality. Robert began to use the phone calls playfully, identifying himself as "Dr. Zhivago." This was in part a humorous parody of the therapist's name, but at the same time it represented a verbally symbolic statement of wished-for oneness with the healing aspects of the therapist. The playfulness then gave way to humorless, relentless intrusiveness, and at the same time the frequency of the calls increased. The hostility of the calls was then interpreted in terms of the patient's growing awareness of and resentment about his separateness from the therapist. At that point the telephoning ceased.

In this phase of therapy, verbal interpretation was offered for the first time in the course of the work. The patient had given some evidence of the capacity for causative, verbally symbolized thought. "Being with you" was identified by the patient as the source of anxiety. The patient was attempting to use speech and symbolic thought for the mastery of anxiety. In the initial interpretation, the patient's upsurge of psychotic symptomatology was formulated as a reflection of the strain arising from the patient's efforts to contain his own experience and thought. Observation of the patient's responses to the initial interpretation, as well as analysis of the countertransference, led to the second group of interventions described in which the therapist interpreted the illusion of curative merger that had emerged in response to the initial interpretation.

The therapist's relation to the illusion that his mind and voice could absorb and render safe the patient's insanity is analogous to the good-enough mother's relation to the illusion of the magically comforting powers of the transitional objection (Winnicott, 1951). The mother's "belief" in the transitional object is genuinely felt, and yet it is not a delusion and is not violently forced upon her by the infant. She believes because the infant believes, and both are on their way to no longer believing. Neither the mother of the infant in the transitional-object stage nor the therapist in the third clinical phase of therapy experiences this as an assault on their hold on reality; the sharing of the illusion is not at all complete and is quite smoothly integrated into the ordinary functioning of their larger personality systems.

Fourth Clinical Phase

As the therapy progressed, three developments were observed to be proceeding concurrently: (1) the patient's capacity for containment of his own thoughts and feelings was expanding, leading to more frequent periods of anxiety, which were becoming increasingly defined and verbally symbolized; (2) his reliance on projective identification as a mode of communication, form of defense, and type of interpersonal relatedness was diminishing; and (3) the therapist more frequently verbalized aspects of his formerly "silent" interpretations.

Toward the end of the second year of therapy, Robert evidenced a dramatic change in his behavior and psychological state. Within the space of several weeks, he began to talk incessantly, but not in a pressured way. He found interest and excitement in almost every detail of life, particularly in the varieties of emotion that could arise between himself and others. For the previous two years, Robert's verbalizations had been restricted almost entirely to very brief phrases or sentences, which were spoken softly, indistinctly, and with very little affect. The sound of Robert's voice in sustained speech had been unknown to the therapist until this time. Now the patient talked almost without interruption for entire sessions at a time. The therapist had a feeling of being with a person who was introducing himself, despite the fact that the patient and therapist had spent more than 500 hours alone together over the previous two years. Robert did not talk directly about the change that had occurred in him, but the therapist, when invited to participate in what felt like a celebration, commented again and again on the sound of Robert's voice, which had become a symbol of his separateness and capacity for independent thought and behavior. (In retrospect, this symbol had been developing over the entire course of the therapy.)

Robert became very concerned about what people's jobs or roles or positions were. He would then insist that they behave in conformity with that definition. Bus routes, train schedules, and street maps (in braille) became the focus of intense interest and a source of pride as the patient became an "authority" on these matters. Emotions and judgments were given shadings, subtlety, and complexity that they had previously lacked. Robert's capacity to learn in a school setting increased dramatically and within several months reached the point where he was able to take remedial classes five days a week at a local community college while living at a halfway house.

There were also frequent occasions when the volume of verbiage reached the point that the sentences the patient spoke became a drone that no longer seemed to be used to communicate ideas. Similarly, questions addressed to the therapist were very often not intended to elicit thoughts or information; instead, the questions were rhetorical, and there was not even a pause in the patient's rhythm of speech for a response to be given.

Interactions were initiated primarily for the pleasure to be found in discovering what kind of jam or fix he could create using the other person almost as he would use a set of paints, with its unique complement of textures and colors. For example, Robert became immersed in vigorous campaigning (telephone canvassing and leaflet distributing) in support of a state referendum that he neither favored nor fully understood.

The therapist was sometimes used as one of these "paint sets" but was more often used as an audience to whom unedited, verbatim recollections could be presented for the purpose of enjoying once again the ordinary day-to-day events of his life that were now found to be so pleasurable. There was a feeling that it would have been a shame to experience these events only once. The patient recounted and demonstrated feelings of self-righteous outrage, sage cynicism, condescending pity, etc. There was a sense of freedom and excitement in all of this. Robert frequently demonstrated arrogance in his relations with other people, which at times reached the point of almost ludicrous disregard for the feelings, rights, and property of others.

Robert experienced a feeling of "power" accruing from his newly achieved level of self-definition and autonomy. For example, in the initial school classes, he would demand that a certain topic be covered on a given day; if the teacher refused to comply, Robert would leave the class, saying, "If you're not going to teach me what I need to learn, I don't have to stay and waste my time." As the therapist listened to accounts of this sort of behavior again and again, he became firmly aware of the fact that for the first time Robert had it fully within his power to flee from the therapy if he so chose. It was not unrealistic of the therapist to feel that there was some risk of this occurring if the patient's fear of his own wishes to reenter symbiotic dependency upon the therapist became too intense. However, the therapist was at the same time aware that his anxiety over the patient's power to flee from the therapy reflected his own, as well as the patient's, reluctance to give up the illusion of mutual ownership involved in symbiotic transference and countertransference.

That an object tie to the therapist had begun to be established was clearly evident, particularly just before breaks in therapy. The patient treated as ridiculous the suggestion that he was disappointed and angry because of the therapist's upcoming vacation. Yet upon leaving the therapy hours during the period before this vacation, Robert was seen using his cane to hit the back of a city bus with great force as it pulled out from the bus stop. While the therapist was away, Robert would loudly and repeatedly proclaim that he was vastly relieved to be freed of the burden of his daily appointments with the therapist. At the same time, he would openly and sadistically taunt the less integrated of the therapist's patients (in the same halfway house) by constantly reminding them of the therapist's absence in the process of asserting his own feelings of freedom and relief.

Some months later, Robert reported memories of childhood events for the first time. There was an intense sense of secretiveness about this. The patient would reveal only one memory fragment in a session and then cut himself off, saying that that was all the therapist was going to learn about the patient. The most guarded of these secrets were memories of his mother. These memories were consciously disguised and censored before being revealed and were permeated by feelings of intense protectiveness of her from fantasied condemnation by the therapist. Also for the first time, the patient began to acknowledge openly the fact of his blindness, although anxiety, fearfulness, the feeling of the unfairness of it, etc. were all conspicuously absent from his matter-of-fact references to his progressive loss of sight. However, he now used his cane to smash every telephone pole and lamp post that he passed, and by this time its tip and handle were broken, while the shaft was becoming increasingly mangled.

This phase of therapy had the unmistakable quality of an advance to a new level of psychological organization and interpersonal relatedness. I would understand the patient during this period as experiencing a combination of the strain of erecting a form of manic defense,[10] as well as the genuine excitement of Mahler's (1972) "practicing subphase" of separation-individuation wherein the infant becomes "intoxicated with its own faculties and with the greatness of the world" (p. 336).

As in previous stages, aspects of the increasingly ambivalent symbiotic transference continued alongside of accumulated gains in the achievement of differentiated object-relatedness. Earlier

[10]The term *manic defense* refers to an unconscious effort to defensively ward off depressive feelings of loss, dependency, and vulnerability. This is achieved by means of assertions of control over and contempt for others. If the other person is felt to be controlled, then one cannot be deserted by him; if the other person is seen as despicable, then his loss does not matter (Klein, 1940; Segal, 1964).

themes of invading and being invaded by other people (or parts of self and object) now took the form of the patient's active interpersonal intrusiveness, which was enacted primarily with words in the context of more differentiated object relations. However, in this phase, the limitation of the capacity to attribute meaning to experience (including painful experience), present and past, was significantly lifted. There was the feeling of release from years of self-imposed sensory deprivation. Feelings, especially those arising from interactions with others, seemed to be freshly discovered. There was immense satisfaction in delineating and clarifying the details, boundaries, and shadings of self- and object-representations and the relation between them.

Equally important was the patient's increased capacity to experience and contain painful thoughts and feelings. His earlier mode of defense had taken the form of a massive shutdown of the capacity to endow present and past perception with meaning, with the result that present perception and memory existed as raw sensory data, things in themselves that were not experienced. In the stage of nonexperience, feelings and thoughts concerning the therapist's vacations, the patient's blindness and its development, and memories of his mother were not defended against by means of removal from conscious awareness (denial or repression), by being disguised as their opposites (reaction formation, idealization, or manic defense), by being attributed to another person (projection or displacement), or by other modes of rearrangement of meaning within the sphere of psychological representation. Such defenses involve rendering the painful meanings dynamically unconscious which, as Freud (1915a) pointed out, is never an entirely successful procedure. Inevitably and inescapably, the unconscious meaning is experienced in some derivative form, in dreams, symptoms, slips, involuntary modifications of one's behavior, inexplicable or overly intense feeling-states, etc. The hallmark of the phase of nonexperience resulting from limitation of capacity to attribute meaning to present and past perceptions is the absence of such derivatives. Meanings are not disguised or removed from awareness; instead, experience is denuded of meaning and the process of generating new meanings is paralyzed. Without meanings, there can be no derivative meanings.

In contrast, in the last phase of therapy described, this limitation had been to some extent lifted, as was reflected in the patient's prominent use of denial, displacement, projection, and isolation of affect in relation to separation from the therapist, the patient's blindness, and his memories of his mother. Although the patient vehemently denied that the therapist's vacation meant anything to him save welcome relief, derivatives of his unconsciously maintained meanings (mental representations of the therapist and himself colored by feelings of anger and loss) were evident in the violent attack on the departing bus and in the way in which he relentlessly and sadistically reminded "weaker" patients of the therapist's absence. Similarly, the patient's matter-of-fact acknowledgment of his blindness, together with the mangling of his cane, reflects the fact that his anger about being blind had not been denuded of meaning and continued to exist in the psychological sphere, albeit in a form in which affect was isolated from conscious thought. Moreover, Robert's hostile feelings toward his mother were no longer empty of meaning and were managed by means of displacement and projection onto the therapist (as opposed to projective identification), indicating that shifts within the sphere of psychological representations were being defensively utilized in an effective way. The therapist could now draw the patient's attention to these derivatives in the course of what was becoming more of a joint effort (of two separate people) at understanding the patient's present and past experience. The patient's use of defensive operations within the representational sphere had not, however, entirely supplanted his efforts at defense by means of destroying meaning and thought. In this regard, the patient's droning can be viewed as representative of an unconscious effort to drain language of its symbolic and communicative value.

IMPLICATIONS FOR CLINICAL THEORY

There are important consequences of the distinctions being made in this chapter between shifts within the representational sphere and changes involving actualization beyond the sphere of psychological representation. Many psychoanalytic concepts have been defined exclusively in terms of changes within the representational sphere and, as a result, fail to include facets of the phenomena they address that lie beyond that sphere. The classical view of transference (Freud, 1912a, 1914a, 1915d) focuses on the modification of the patient's psychic representation of the analyst (or another person) in congruence with features of the conscious and unconscious representation of an internalized past object relationship. The patient *displaces* and *projects* feelings and ideas derived from previous significant relationships (often from childhood) onto present object-representations (Moore and Fine, 1968; Rycroft, 1973). Giovacchini states that "The essence of transference in psychoanalysis is the projection of the infantile, or relatively infantile elements onto the mental representation of the therapist" (1975, p. 15).[11] Thus, transference has been formulated in terms of the mental operations of one person, that is, as an intrapsychic event. A person alone in a room can project (or displace) feelings derived from a previous relationship onto an imaginary person (or hallucinated image), a movie star, a political figure, a personified government agency (for example, the FBI), etc. This conception of transference does not require that a second personality system either be affected by or have influence upon the process.

Fairbairn (1944, 1946) sharpened the analytic conception of what it is that is repeated in the transference by pointing out that

---

[11]Despite Giovacchini's view of transference as a form of projection, he operationally uses the concept as a two-person phenomenon in which "the patient projects his rudimentary organized self *into* the analyst. When he once more incorporates it as his own, there has been a realignment of various parts of the self that permit further development" (1975, p. 32, italics added).

it is not objects, nor object-representations, that are internalized; rather, it is a representation of the *self in relation to the object* that is internalized, in addition to the specific affective link that characterizes the relationship. The work of Balint (1968), Bion (1959b), Boyer (1978), Giovacchini (1975), Khan (1974), Klein (1946, 1955), Langs (1978), M. Little (1966), Racker (1968), Rosenfeld (1952b), Sandler (1976b), Searles (1963), Winnicott (1947), and others has led to a widening of the original focus of the concept to include not only the idea of a shift in the psychological representation of the analyst but also an *interpersonal enactment* of that representational shift in the form of pressure exerted on the therapist to experience himself and to behave in a manner congruent with the self-and/or object-representation depicted in the internalized relationship. This is a conception of transference as a phenomenon requiring the interaction of two separate personality systems. Translated into the terms that I have been using, transference is understood by these analysts as necessarily involving interpersonal actualization.

I am proposing that the analytic formulation of transferences encountered in work with schizophrenic patients be widened still further to encompass an additional facet of the phenomenon that is inherent in Fairbairn's contribution but has not yet been sufficiently recognized: transference may also involve a form of intrapersonal actualization, wherein the person modifies his own psychological capacities (and not simply his self- and/or object-representations) in congruence with features of the self- and/or object-representation in the earlier object relationship. In other words, the patient limits his psychological capacities in the transference to conform to the ego state represented in the internalized object relationship. Transference is thus conceptualized in terms of three interrelated facets: (1) the projection of an internal self- and/or object-representation onto the psychic representation of the therapist (an intrapsychic event); (2) the interpersonal actualization of that fantasy such that the therapist is exposed to interpersonal pressure to conform to the unconscious projective fantasy (projective identification); and (3) the patient's limitation of his own psychological capacities in congruence with the state of his ego as depicted in the internalized object relationship (an intrapersonal actualization).

From this perspective, there is also a need to broaden the psychoanalytic formulation of resistance. Resistance was seen by Freud (1923) as the manifestation of the patient's opposition to becoming aware of dynamically unconscious meanings (see also LaPlanche & Pontalis, 1973). The concept has been broadened by others to include all manifestations of the patient's opposition to psychological growth (Schafer, 1973). In this latter tradition, I would propose that resistance be understood as also involving the patient's opposition to change in his capacity for thought and experience, that is, opposition directed against enlarging the functioning of formerly limited capacities that exist on a level superordinate to that of repressed meanings. Opposition to an ending of a limitation of psychological capacities for thought and experience are equally a manifestation of resistance as the patient's opposition to the uncovering of the repressed. In other words, the schizophrenic not only resists awareness of meanings, but also resists creating and maintaining both conscious and unconscious meanings and representations. It is the latter form of resistance that has led to the schizophrenic so often being declared ego-defective and unanalyzable (A. Freud, 1976; Kohut, 1977; London, 1973a, 1973b; Wexler, 1971).

SUMMARY

In this chapter, I have described aspects of the first three years of the psychonalytic treatment of a blind, schizophrenic patient. After an initial period of progressively diminishing psychotic symptomatology, the patient developed a mode of behaving and relating that was more like that of a "creature" than of a person. However, there was nothing to indicate that the patient felt like or had fantasies of being a "creature." The therapist noted that he himself felt neither the compassion nor the revulsion that he ordinarily experienced in the course of working with severly regressed schizophrenic patients.

After about a year, the patient began almost imperceptibly to become present, to exist in a way that created discernible and sustained forms of interpersonal pressure. The qualities of the pressure were diffuse and initially were entirely in the form of sensory impingements on the therapist (unlabeled odors, sounds, and sights). Only gradually were the patient and therapist able to learn about the specific meanings of these impingements. In fact, the capacity to endow sensory data with meaning was precisely what had been absent in the first year of work. In the second year, through the therapist's "processing" of the patient's predominantly nonverbal productions as well as the accompanying countertransference feelings, the patient increasingly became able to endow with meaning his formerly diffuse, sensory-level experiential state. These unfolding meanings centered around the patient's conflicted rebellion against feelings of being symbiotically suffused or "haunted."

In the latter half of the second year and in the third year of therapy, the patient progressively developed the capacity to experience and contain his own feelings and thoughts. There was an initial retreat from such containment in the form of an illusion (in which the therapist was subtly invited to participate) that the therapist and patient were not quite separate and that the therapist's voice could render safe the patient's insane thoughts and feelings. Gradually, as this was interpreted, the patient began to experience the exhilaration and feeling of power involved in conceiving of himself as a person with the capacity to think, feel, and act. This excitement also reflected a form of manic defense erected against feelings of loss, abandonment, and powerlessness that are inevitable accompaniments of awareness of one's separateness. These defenses occasionally became overtaxed, and brief periods of psychotic regression would ensue with partial loss of self–object differentiation. These regressions offered further opportunity to rework the many incompletely resolved aspects of the previous phases of work.

I feel that the clinical phenomena described in this case report could not be formulated adequately by relying exclusively on formulations involving either intrapersonal or interpersonal shifts or changes in the patient's utilization of his mental capacities. The task of this volume has been to develop the beginnings of a conceptual framework to describe, organize, and think about the various forms of interplay among these spheres. The concept of actualization was introduced in order to afford a way of talking about transformations from the representational sphere into one of the other spheres. Projective identification can then be thought of as a form of actualization: unconscious fantasies are actualized by the evocation of congruent feelings in another person. Similarly, intrapersonal actualization refers to the way in which schizophrenic patients not only imagine mental catastrophies but actually bring about and maintain severe limitations of their own capacities for experience and thought. This sometimes reaches the point of an almost complete psychological shutdown, which I have termed a state of nonexperience.

References

Abraham, K. (1922). The spider as a dream symbol. In *Selected Papers of Karl Abraham,* trans. D. Bryan and A. Strachey, pp. 326–332. London: Hogarth Press, 1927.

Adler, G. (1973). Hospital treatment of borderline patients. *American Journal of Psychiatry* 130:32–36.

Altshul, V. (1980). The hateful therapist and the countertransference psychosis. *National Association of Private Psychiatric Hospitals Journal* 11:15–23.

Arlow, J., and Brenner, C. (1964). *Psychoanalytic Concepts and the Structural Theory.* New York: International Universities Press.

——— (1969). The psychopathology of the psychoses: a proposed revision. *International Journal of Psycho-Analysis* 50:5–14.

Balint, M. (1952). *Primary Love and Psychoanalytic Technique.* New York: Livewright, 1965.

——— (1968). *The Basic Fault.* London: Tavistock.

Benedek, T. (1973). *Psychoanalytic Investigations.* New York: Quadrangle/New York Times Book Company.

Bion, W. R. (1955). Language and the schizophrenic. In *New Directions in Psycho-Analysis,* ed. M. Klein, P. Heimann, and R. Money-Kyrle, pp. 220–329. London: Tavistock.

——— (1956). Development of schizophrenic thought. *International Journal of Psycho-Analysis* 37:344–346.

——— (1959a). *Experiences in Groups.* New York: Basic Books.

——— (1959b). Attacks on linking. *International Journal of Psycho-Analysis* 40:308–315.

——— (1962a). A theory of thinking. *International Journal of Psycho-Analysis* 43:306–310.

——— (1962b). *Learning from Experience.* New York: Basic Books.

——— (1967). *Second Thoughts.* New York: Jason Aronson.

——— (1977a). *Seven Servants.* New York: Jason Aronson.

——— (1977b). Unpublished presentation at Children's Hospital, San Francisco, California.

Boyer, L. B. (1978). Countertransference experiences with extremely regressed patients. In *Countertransference,* eds. L. Epstein and A. Feiner. New York: Jason Aronson. 1979.

——— and Giovacchini, P. L. (1967). *Psychoanalytic Treatment of Schizophrenic and Characterological Disorders.* New York: Jason Aronson.

Brodey, W. M. (1965). On the dynamics of narcissism: I. Externalization and early ego development. *The Psychoanalytic Study of the Child* 20:165–193.

Bullard, D. (1940). The organization of psychoanalytic procedure in the hospital. *Journal of Nervous and Mental Disorders* 91:697–703.

Bush, M. (1981). Personal communication.

Caudill, W. (1958). *The Psychiatric Hospital as a Small Society.* Cambridge: Harvard University Press.

Donnet, J. L., and Green, A. (1973). *L'Enfant de Ca. Psychanalyse d'un entretien. La Psychose blanche.* Paris: Editions Minuit.

Edelson, M. (1970). *Sociotherapy and Psychotherapy.* Chicago: University of Chicago Press.

Engel, G. L., Reichsman, F., and Segal, H., (1956). A study of an infant with a gastric fistula. I. Behavior and the rate of total hydrochloric acid secretion. *Psychosomatic Medicine* 18:374–398.

Erikson, E. (1978). Personal Communication.

Fairbairn, W. R. D. (1940). Schizoid factors in the personality. In *Psychoanalytic Studies of the Personality* pp. 3–27. London: Routledge and Kegan Paul, 1952.

——— (1944). Endopsychic structure considered in terms of object-relationships. In *Psychoanalytic Studies of the Personality* pp. 82–136. London: Routledge and Kegan Paul, 1952.

——— (1946). Object-relationships and dynamic structure. In *Psychoanalytic Studies of the Personality* pp. 137–151. London: Routledge and Kegan Paul, 1952.

——— (1952). *An Object-Relations Theory of the Personality.* New York: Basic Books. (*Psychoanalytic Studies of the Personality.* London: Routledge and Kegan Paul.)

Fraiberg, S., Adelson, E., and Shapiro, V. (1975). Ghosts in the nursery: a psychoanalytic approach to impaired infant–mother relationships. *Journal of the American Academy of Child Psychiatry* 14:387–421.

Freeman, T. (1953). Some problems in inpatient psychotherapy in a neurosis unit. In *The Therapeutic Community,* ed. M. Jones, pp. 69–84, New York: Basic Books.

——— (1970). The psychopathology of the psychoses: a reply to Arlow and Brenner. *International Journal of Psycho-Analysis* 51:407–415.

Freud, A. (1936). *The Ego and the Mechanisms of Defense.* New York: International Universities Press, 1965.

——— (1976). Changes in psychoanalytic practice and experience. *International Journal of Psycho-Analysis* 57:257–260.

Freud, S. (1894). The neuro-psychoses of defence. Standard Edition 3.

——— (1895). Draft H: Paranoia. In *The Origins of Psycho-Analysis,* ed. M. Bonaparte, A. Freud, and E. Kris. New York: Basic Books, 1954.

——— (1896). Further remarks on the neuro-psychoses of defence. Standard Edition 3.

——— (1900). *The Interpretation of Dreams.* Standard Edition 4/5.

——— (1905). *Three Essays on the Theory of Sexuality.* Standard Edition 7.

——— (1910). The future prospects of psycho-analytic therapy. Standard Edition 11.

——— (1911). Psycho-analytic notes on an autobiographical account of a case of paranoia (dementia paranoides). Standard Edition 12.

——— (1912a). The dynamics of transference. Standard Edition 12.

——— (1912b). Recommendations to physicians practicing psycho-analysis. Standard Edition 12.

——— (1913). On beginning the treatment. Standard Edition 12.

——— (1914a). Remembering, repeating and working through. Standard Edition 12.

——— (1914b). On narcissism: an introduction. Standard Edition 14.

——— (1914c). On the history of the psycho-analytic movement. Standard Edition 14.

——— (1915a). Instincts and their vicissitudes. Standard Edition 14.

——— (1915b). Mourning and melancholia. Standard Edition 14.

——— (1915c). The unconscious. Standard Edition 14.

——— (1915d). Observations on transference love. Standard Edition 12.

——— (1915e). Repression. Standard Edition 14.

——— (1917). A metapsychological supplement to the theory of dreams. Standard Edition 14.

——— (1920). *Beyond the Pleasure Principle.* Standard Edition 18.

——— (1923). *The Ego and the Id.* Standard Edition 19.

——— (1924a). Neurosis and psychosis. Standard Edition 19.

——— (1924b). The loss of reality in neurosis and psychosis. Standard Edition 19.

——— (1926). The question of lay analysis. Standard Edition 20.

——— (1927). Fetishism. Standard Edition 21.

——— (1937). Analysis terminable and interminable. Standard Edition 23.

Fromm-Reichmann, F. (1937). Problems of therapeutic management in a psychiatric hospital. *Psychoanalytic Quarterly* 16:325–356.

——— (1950). *Principles of Intensive Psychotherapy.* Chicago: University of Chicago Press.

Giovacchini, P. L. (1975). Various aspects of the analytic process. In *Tactics and Techniques in Psychoanalytic Therapy,* vol. 2, ed. P. L. Giovacchini, pp. 5–95. New York: Jason Aronson.

——— (1979). *Treatment of Primitive Mental States.* New York: Jason Aronson.

——— (1980). Primitive agitation and primal confusion. In *Schizophrenic, Borderline, and Characterological Disorders,* ed. L. B. Boyer and P. L. Giovacchini. New York: Jason Aronson.

Gitelson, M. (1952). The emotional position of the analyst in the psycho-analytic situation. *International Journal of Psycho-Analysis* 33:1–10.

Glover, E. (1931). The therapeutic effect of inexact interpretation. *International Journal of Psycho-Analysis* 12:397–411.

——— (1955). *The Technique of Psychoanalysis.* New York: International Universities Press.

Graber, G. H. (1925). Die schwarze spinne: menschheitsentwicklung nach Jeremais Gotthelfs gleichnamiger novelle, dargestallt unter besonderer berucksihtigungder rolle der frau. *Imago* 11:254–334. (Trans. S. Ruddy and C. Michel, unpublished.)

Green, A. (1975). The analyst, symbolization and absence in the analytic setting (On changes in analytic practice and analytic experience). *International Journal of Psycho-Analysis* 56:1–22.

——— (1977). The borderline concept. In *Borderline Personality Disorders,* ed. P. Hartocollis, pp. 15–44. New York: International Universities Press.

Greenacre, P. (1959). Focal symbiosis. In *Dynamic Psychopathology in Childhood,* ed. L. Jessner and E. Pavenstedt, pp. 240–256, New York: Grune and Stratton.

Greenblatt, M., Levinson, D. and Williams, R. (1957). *The Patient and the Mental Hospital.* Glencoe, Ill.: Free Press.

Greenson, R. (1967). *The Technique and Practice of Psychoanalysis.* New York: International Universities Press.

Grinberg, L. (1962). On a specific aspect of countertransference due to the patient's projective identification. *International Journal of Psycho-Analysis* 43:436–440.

Grotstein, J. S. (1977a). The psychoanalytic concept of schizophrenia: I. The dilemma. *International Journal of Psycho-Analysis* 58:403–425.

——— (1977b). The psychoanalytic concept of schizophrenia: II. Reconciliation. *International Journal of Psycho-Analysis* 58:427–452.

——— (1979). Demoniacal possession, splitting, and the torment of joy. *Contemporary Psychoanalysis* 15:407–445.

Guntrip, H. (1961). *Personality Structure and Human Interaction.* New York: International Universities Press.

——— (1969). *Schizoid Phenomena, Object Relations and the Self.* New York: International Universities Press.

Hartmann, H. (1939). *Ego Psychology and the Problem of Adaptation,* New York: International Universities Press, 1958.

——— (1953). Contribution to the metapsychology of schizophrenia. In *Essays on Ego Psychology,* pp. 177–198. New York: International Universities Press, 1964.

Heimann, P. (1950). On counter-transference. *International Journal of Psycho-Analysis* 31:81–84.

Jacobson, E. (1964). *The Self and the Object World.* New York: International Universities Press.

Jones, M. (1953). *The Therapeutic Community.* New York: Basic Books.

Kehoe, M., and Ironside, W. (1963). Studies on the experimental evocation of depressive responses during hypnosis. II. The influence of depressive responses upon the secretion of gastric acid. *Psychosomatic Medicine* 25:403–419.

Kernberg, O. (1966). Structural derivatives of object relations. *International Journal of Psycho-Analysis* 47:236–253.

——— (1968). The treatment of patients with borderline personality organization. *International Journal of Psycho-Analysis* 49:600–619.

——— (1976). Normal and pathological development. In *Object Relations Theory and Clincial Psychoanalysis,* pp. 55–84. New York: Jason Aronson.

Khan, M. M. R. (1963). The concept of cumulative trauma. *Psychoanalytic Study of the Child* 18:286–306.

——— (1969). On symbiotic omnipotence. In *The Privacy of the Self,* pp. 82–92. New York: International Universities Press, 1974.

——— (1974). *The Privacy of the Self.* New York: International Universities Press.

——— (1975). Introduction. *Through Paediatrics to Psycho-Analysis,* D. W. Winnicott. New York: Basic Books.

Klein, M. (1940). Mourning and its relation to manic-depressive states. In *Contributions to Psycho-Analysis, 1921-1945,* pp. 311–338. London: Hogarth Press.

——— (1946). Notes on some schizoid mechanisms. In *Envy and Gratitude and Other Works, 1946–1963,* pp. 1–24. New York: Delacorte Press/Seymour Laurence, 1975.

——— (1948). *The Psycho-Analysis of Children.* London: Hogarth Press.

——— (1955). On identification. In *Envy and Gratitude and Other Works, 1946–1963,* pp. 141–175. New York: Delacorte Press/Seymour Laurence, 1975.

——— (1961). *Narrative of a Child Analysis.* New York: Basic Books.

Knight, R. (1936). Psychoanalysis of hospitalized patients. *Bulletin of the Menninger Clinic* 1:158–167.

——— (1940). Introjection, projection and identification. *Psychoanalytic Quarterly* 9:334–341.

Kohut, H. (1971). *The Analysis of the Self.* New York: International Universities Press.

——— (1977). *The Restoration of the Self.* New York: International Universities Press.

Kubie, L. (1967). The relation of psychotic disorganization to the neurotic process. *Journal of the American Psychoanalytic Association* 15:626–640.

Laing, R. D. (1959). *The Divided Self.* Baltimore: Pelican, 1965.

Langs, R. (1975). Therapeutic misalliances. *International Journal of Psychoanalytic Psychotherapy* 4:77–105.

——— (1976). *The Bipersonal Field.* New York: Jason Aronson.

——— (1978). *The Listening Process.* New York: Jason Aronson.

LaPlanche, J., and Pontalis, J. B. (1973). *The Language of Psycho-Analysis.* New York: W. W. Norton.

Lerner, S. (1979). The excessive need to treat: a countertherapeutic force in psychiatric hospital treatment. *Bulletin of the Menninger Clinic* 43:463–471.

Lifton, R. J. (1979). Schizophrenia—lifeless life. In *The Broken Connection,* ed. R. J. Lifton, pp. 222–238. New York: Simon and Schuster.

Little, M. (1958). On delusional transference (transference psychosis). *International Journal of Psycho-Analysis* 39:134–138.

——— (1961). Countertransference and the patient's response to it. *International Journal of Psycho-Analysis* 32:32–40.

——— (1966). Transference in borderline states. *International Journal of Psycho-Analysis* 47:476–485.

Little, R. (1966). Oral aggression in spider legends. *American Imago* 23:169–179.

——— (1967). Spider phobias. *The Psychoanalytic Quarterly* 36:51–60.

Loewald, H. (1962). Internalization, separation, mourning and the superego. *Psychoanalytic Quarterly* 31:483–504.

——— (1971). On motivation and instinct theory. *The Psychoanalytic Study of the Child* 26:91–128.

London, N. (1973a) An essay on psychoanalytic theory: two theories of schizophrenia. Part I: Review and critical assessment of the development of the two theories. *International Journal of Psycho-Analysis* 54:169–178.

——— (1973b). An essay on psychoanalytic theory: two theories of schizophrenia. Part II: Discussion and restatement of the specific theory of schizophrenia. *International Journal of Psycho-Analysis* 54:179–193.

Mahler, M. (1952). On child psychosis and schizophrenia: autistic and symbiotic infantile psychoses. *Psychoanalytic Study of the Child* 7:286–305.

——— (1968). *On Human Symbiosis and the Vicissitudes of Individuation.* New York: International Universities Press.

——— (1972). On the first three subphases of the separation–individuation process. *International Journal of Psycho-Analysis* 53:333–338.

Malin, A., and Grotstein, J. (1966). Projective identification in the therapeutic process. *International Journal of Psycho-Analysis* 47:26–31.

Maltsburger, T., and Buie, D. (1974). Countertransference hate in the treatment of suicidal patients. *Archives of General Psychiatry* 30:625–633.

McDougall, J. (1974). The psychosoma and the psychoanalytic process. *International Review of Psycho-Analysis* 1:437–459.

Meissner, W. W. (1980). A note on projective identification. *Journal of the American Psychoanalytic Association* 28:43–67.

Menninger, W. C. (1936). Psychoanalytic principles applied to the treatment of hospitalized patients. *Bulletin of the Menninger Clinic* 1:35–43.

Moore, B., and Fine, B. (1968). *A Glossary of Psychoanalytic Terms and Concepts.* New York: American Psychoanalytic Association.

Nadelson, T. (1976). Victim, victimizer: interaction in the psychotherapy of borderline patients. *International Journal of Psychoanalytic Psychotherapy* 5:115–129.

Nelson, M.C., Nelson, B., Sherman, M., and Strean, H. (1968). *Roles and Paradigms in Psychotherapy.* New York: Grune and Stratton.

Ogden, T. H. (1974). A psychoanalytic psychotherapy of a patient with cerebral palsy: the relation of aggression to self-and body-representations. *International Journal of Psychoanalytic Psychotherapy* 3:419–433.

——— (1976). Psychological unevenness in the academically successful student. *International Journal of Psychoanalytic Psychotherapy* 5:437–448.

——— (1978a). A developmental view of identifications resulting from maternal impingements. *International Journal of Psychoanalytic Psychotherapy* 7:486–507.

——— (1978b). A reply to Dr. Ornston's discussion of "Identifications resulting from maternal impingements." *International Journal of Psychoanalytic Psychotherapy* 7:528–532.

——— (1979). On projective identification. *International Journal of Psycho-Analysis* 60:357–373.

——— (1980). On the nature of schizophrenic conflict. *International Journal of Psycho-Analysis* 61:513–533.

——— (1981). Projective identification in psychiatric hospital treatment. *Bulletin of the Menninger Clinic* 45:317–333.

Ornston, D. (1978). Projective identification and maternal impingement. *International Journal of Psychoanalytic Psychotherapy* 7:508–528.

Pao, P. (1973). Notes on Freud's theory of schizophrenia. *International Journal of Psycho-Analysis* 54:469–476.

Parsons, T. (1937). *The Structure of Social Action.* New York: Free Press of Glencoe.

——— (1951). *The Social System.* New York: Free Press of Glencoe.

——— (1957). The mental hospital as a type of organization. In *The Patient and the Mental Hospital,* ed. M. Greenblatt, D. Levinson, and R. Williams, pp. 108–129. Glencoe, Ill.: Free Press.

Racker, H. (1957). The Meanings and Uses of Countertransference. *Psychoanalytic Quarterly* 26:303–357.

——— (1968). *Transference and Countertransference.* New York: International Universities Press.

Reich, A. (1951). On counter-transference. *International Journal of Psycho-Analysis* 32:25–31.

——— (1960). Further remarks on counter-transference. *International Journal of Psycho-Analysis* 41:389–395.

——— (1966). *Psychoanalytic Contributions.* New York: International Universities Press.

Reider, N. (1936). Hospital care of patients undergoing psychoanalysis. *Bulletin of the Menninger Clinic* 1:168–175.

Ritvo, S., and Solnit, A. J. (1958). Influences of early mother–child interaction on identification processes. *Psychoanalytic Study of the Child* 13:64–85.

Rosenfeld, H. (1952a). Transference-phenomena and transference-analysis in the acute catatonic schizophrenic. *International Journal of Psycho-Analysis* 33:457–464.

——— (1952b). Notes on the psycho-analysis of the superego conflict of an acute schizophrenic patient. *International Journal of Psycho-Analysis* 33:111–131.

——— (1954). Considerations regarding the psycho-analytic approach to acute and chronic schizophrenia. *International Journal of Psycho-Analysis* 35:135–140.

——— (1965). *Psychotic States.* New York: International Universities Press.

Rycroft, C. (1973). *A Critical Dictionary of Psycho-Analysis.* Towata, N.J.: Littlefield Adams.

Sandler, J. (1976a). Dreams, unconscious fantasies and "identity of perception." *International Review of Psycho-Analysis* 3:33–42.

——— (1976b). Countertransference and role responsiveness. *International Review of Psycho-Analysis* 3:43–47.

——— and Sandler, A.-M. (1978). On the development of object relationships and affect. *International Journal of Psycho-Analysis* 59:285–296.

Schafer, R. (1959). Generative empathy in the treatment situation. *The Psychoanalytic Quarterly* 28:342–373.

——— (1968). *Aspects of Internalization.* New York: International Universities Press.

——— (1973). The idea of resistance. *International Journal of Psycho-Analysis* 54:259–285.

——— (1974). Personal communication.

——— (1976). *A New Language for Psychoanalysis.* New Haven: Yale University Press.

Searles, H. (1959). Oedipal love in the countertransference. In *Collected Papers on Schizophrenia and Related Subjects,* pp. 284–303. New York: International Universities Press, 1965.

——— (1963). Transference psychosis in the psychotherapy of schizophrenia. In *Collected Papers on Schizophrenia and Related Subjects,* pp. 654–716. New York: International Universities Press, 1965.

——— (1965). *Collected Papers on Schizophrenia and Related Subjects.* New York: International Universities Press.

——— (1975). The patient as therapist to the analyst. In *Tactics and Techniques in Psychoanalytic Therapy,* vol. 2, ed. P. L. Giovacchini, pp. 95–151. New York: Jason Aronson.

Segal, H. (1957). Notes on symbol formation. *International Journal of Psycho-Analysis* 38:391–397.

——— (1964). *An Introduction to the Work of Melanie Klein.* New York: Basic Books.

——— (1967). Melanie Klein's technique. In *Psychoanalytic Techniques,* ed. B. Wolman, pp. 168–190. New York: Basic Books.

Sherman, M. (1968). Siding with the resistance vs. interpretation: role implications. In *Roles and Paradigms in Psychotherapy,* ed. M. C. Nelson, B. Nelson, M. Sherman, and H. Strean, pp. 74–108. New York: Grune and Stratton.

Simmel, E. (1929). Psycho-analytic treatment in a sanitorium. *International Journal of Psycho-Analysis* 10:70–89.

Spitz, R. (1945). Diacritic and coenesthetic organizations. *Psychoanalytic Review* 32:146–162.

——— (1965). *The First Year of Life.* New York: International Universities Press.

Spotnitz, H. (1969). *Modern Psychoanalysis of the Schizophrenic Patient.* New York: Grune and Stratton.

——— (1976). *Psychotherapy of Pre-Oedipal Conditions.* New York: Jason Aronson.

Stanton, A., and Schwartz, M. (1954). *The Mental Hospital.* New York: Basic Books.

Sterba, R. (1950). On spiders, hanging and oral sadism. *American Imago* 7:21–28.

Stotland, E., and Kobler, A. (1965). *Life and Death of a Mental Hospital.* Seattle: University of Washington Press.

Strean, H. (1968). Paradigmatic interventions in seemingly difficult therapeutic situations. In *Roles and Paradigms in Psychotherapy,* ed. M. C. Nelson, B. Nelson, M. Sherman, and H. Strean, pp. 179–191. New York: Grune and Stratton.

Sullivan, H. S. (1930–1931). Socio-psychiatric research. In *Schizophrenia as a Human Process,* pp. 256–270. New York: W. W. Norton, 1962.

——— (1956). *Clinical Studies in Psychiatry.* New York: W. W. Norton.

Wangh, M. (1962). The "evocation of a proxy": a psychological maneuver, its use as a defense, its purposes and genesis. *The Psychoanalytic Study of the Child* 17:451–472.

Weiss, J. (1971). The emergence of new themes: a contribution to the psychoanalytic theory of therapy. *International Journal of Psychoanalysis* 52:459–467.

———, Sampson, H., Gassner, S., and Caston, J. (1980). Further research on the psychoanalytic process. The Psychotherapy Research Group, Department of Psychiatry, *Mount Zion Hospital and Medical Center Bulletin #4,* June, 1980.

Wexler, M. (1971). Schizophrenia: conflict and deficiency. *Psychoanalytic Quarterly* 40:83–99.

Will, O. A. (1970). The therapeutic use of the self. *Medical Arts and Sciences* 24:3–14.

——— (1975). Schizophrenia: psychological treatment. In *Comprehensive Textbook of Psychiatry,* ed. A. Freedman, H. Kaplan, and B. Sadock, pp. 939–955. Baltimore: Williams and Wilkins.

Winnicott, D. W. (1945). Primitive emotional development. In *Through Paediatrics to Psycho-Analysis,* pp. 145–156. New York: Basic Books, 1975.

——— (1947). Hate in the countertransference. In *Through Paediatrics to Psycho-Analysis,* pp. 194–203. New York: Basic Books, 1975.

——— (1948). Paediatrics and psychiatry. In *Through Paediatrics to Psycho-Analysis,* pp. 157–173. New York: Basic Books, 1975.

——— (1951). Transitional objects and transitional phenomena. In *Through Paediatrics to Psycho-Analysis,* pp. 229–242. New York: Basic Books, 1975.

——— (1952). Psychoses and child care. In *Through Paediatrics to Psycho-Analysis,* pp. 219–228. New York: Basic Books, 1975.

——— (1954). Metapsychological and clinical aspects of regression within the psycho-analytical set-up. In *Through Paediatrics to Psycho-Analysis,* pp. 278–294. New York: Basic Books, 1975.

——— (1956). Primary maternal preoccupation. In *Through Paediatrics to Psycho-Analysis,* pp. 300–305. New York: Basic Books, 1975.

——— (1958). The capacity to be alone. In *Maturational Processes and the Facilitating Environment,* pp. 29–36. New York: International Universities Press, 1965.

——— (1960a). The theory of the parent–infant relationship. In *Maturational Processes and the Facilitating Environment,* pp. 37–55. New York: International Universities Press, 1965.

——— (1960b). Ego Distortion in terms of the true and the false self, pp. 140–152. In *Maturational Processes and the Facilitating Environment.* New York: International Universities Press, 1965.

——— (1963). Dependence in infant-care, in child-care, and in the psycho-analytic setting. In *Maturational Processes and the Facilitating Environment,* pp. 249–260. New York: International Universities Press, 1965.

——— (1967). Mirror-role of mother and family in child development. In *Playing and Reality,* pp. 111–118. New York: Basic Books, 1971.

——— (1971). Interrelating apart from instinctual drive and in terms of cross-identifications. In *Playing and Reality,* pp. 119–137. New York: Basic Books, 1971.

Zinner, J. and Shapiro, R. (1972). Projective identification as a mode of perception and behavior in families of adolescents. *International Journal of Psycho-Analysis* 53:523–530.

Index

Index

Index